FAITH GORSKY AND **LARA CLEVENGER,** MSH, RDN, CPT

KETO BBQ

From Bunless Burgers to Cauliflower "Potato" Salad, 100+ DELICIOUS, LOW-CARB RECIPES FOR A KETO-FRIENDLY BARBECUE

ADAMS MEDIA

NEW YORK   LONDON   TORONTO   SYDNEY   NEW DELHI

Adams Media
An Imprint of Simon & Schuster, Inc.
57 Littlefield Street
Avon, Massachusetts 02322

First Adams Media trade paperback edition May 2021

ADAMS MEDIA and colophon are trademarks of Simon & Schuster.

For information about special discounts for bulk purchases, please contact Simon & Schuster Special Sales at 1-866-506-1949 or business@simonandschuster.com.

The Simon & Schuster Speakers Bureau can bring authors to your live event. For more information or to book an event contact the Simon & Schuster Speakers Bureau at 1-866-248-3049 or visit our website at www.simonspeakers.com.

Interior design by Sylvia McArdle
Photographs by James Stefiuk

Manufactured in the United States of America

1 2021

Library of Congress Cataloging-in-Publication Data
Names: Gorsky, Faith, author. | Clevenger, Lara, author.
Title: Keto BBQ / Faith Gorsky and Lara Clevenger, MSH, RDN, CPT.
Description: First Adams Media trade paperback edition. | Avon, Massachusetts: Adams Media, 2021.
| Series: Keto | Includes index.
Identifiers: LCCN 2021000309 | ISBN 9781507214534 (pb) | ISBN 9781507214541 (ebook)
Subjects: LCSH: Ketogenic diet--Recipes. | Reducing diets--Recipes. | Low-carbohydrate diet--Recipes.
| Barbecuing. | LCGFT: Cookbooks.
Classification: LCC RM237.73 .G67 2021 | DDC 641.5/6383--dc23
LC record available at https://lccn.loc.gov/2021000309

ISBN 978-1-5072-1453-4
ISBN 978-1-5072-1454-1 (ebook)

CONTENTS

CHAPTER 5
CONDIMENTS 38

CHAPTER 6
BARBECUE CHICKEN AND TURKEY 49

CHAPTER 7
BARBECUE PORK 64

CV 02.18.2021 0122

CHAPTER 8

BARBECUE BEEF 74

CHAPTER 9

SAUSAGES AND HOT DOGS 96

CHAPTER 10

BARBECUE SEAFOOD 106

INTRODUCTION

Sticky and sweet barbecue meats. Fluffy corn bread. Sweet tea.

If you thought you'd have to give up all these barbecue favorites just to be successful on the keto diet, think again! *Keto BBQ* will bring barbecue main dishes, sides, and drinks back into your life and give you lots of keto options for both family-friendly meals and guest-worthy backyard barbecues.

Here you'll find more than one hundred keto-approved barbecue recipes to help you refashion your favorite high-carb/high-sugar barbecue foods as delicious keto versions that taste amazing. With this book you'll always have keto recipes on hand so you won't feel deprived at your next barbecue. You'll find keto main dishes like Pulled Pork Sandwiches, Glazed Beef Short Ribs, Grilled Shrimp Po'boys, and Chili-Cheese Dogs. You'll also find barbecue sides like Jalapeño-Cheddar "Corn Bread," Cheddar Cauliflower "Mac" and Cheese, Creamy Coleslaw, and Smoky Guacamole—not to mention tempting desserts like Chocolate Cake with Fudgy Ganache and Pecan Pie Bars.

These keto barbecue dishes will fit easily into your lifestyle and help keep your macros on target with minimal effort. With these recipes, you can enjoy all of your favorite barbecue meals in a low-carb way so you can continue on your path to a better, healthier you!

CHAPTER 1

INTRODUCTION TO KETO BARBECUE

From Memorial Day to Labor Day, picnics, potlucks, and barbecues are a way of life. Grilling and summer just seem to go hand in hand! When you're following a ketogenic lifestyle, it can be difficult to navigate the sweet and sticky goodness that's found everywhere from ribs to wings to sauces. And that's before you even get to the side dishes or desserts! But with some planning ahead, it's easy to transform a sugar- and carb-laden barbecue into a keto-friendly occasion. This book contains just about every barbecue sauce flavor you can dream up, low-carb side dishes and desserts, and even hot dog and hamburger buns. And if dry rubs or marinades are more your style, we have you covered there too. Just bring the meat and heat!

This chapter discusses the ketogenic diet, including what it is, the macronutrient breakdown, how to tell when your body switches over to using ketones for energy, and what to expect when your body is in ketosis. It will also go over keto barbecue basics and give you a list of some of the best keto barbecue tips.

WHAT IS THE KETO DIET?

A keto diet is a low-carbohydrate, moderate-protein, high-fat diet. When you reduce your intake of carbohydrates (your body's usual source of energy), your body is forced to adapt and make ketones to use for energy instead. If you're at a caloric surplus, your body will use these ketones and fatty acids for fuel; but if you're at a caloric deficit, your body will tap into its fat storage and use your existing fat for fuel.

Let's talk about what happens in your body when you eat carbs. Carbohydrate digestion occurs in the gastrointestinal tract, starting in the mouth. First, your body breaks the carbs down into glucose, which then enters the bloodstream through the small intestine, causing blood glucose (blood sugar) to rise. This rise in blood sugar triggers a secretion of insulin, which transports glucose from your blood into your cells so it can be used as energy. When you eat more carbohydrates than your body needs for fuel, the excess is stored as fat in the form of triglycerides.

However, when your carb intake is limited, your body must turn to alternative fuel sources. First your body will use its stored glucose (called glycogen) from the muscles and liver. After that, it will break down fat for energy. That fat comes either from your diet or from fat stored in the form of fatty acids and ketones (also called ketone bodies). Even when your carb intake is limited, your body runs on a combination of glucose, ketones, and fatty acids, because your body continues to produce glucose through a process called gluconeogenesis. Because our bodies are able to produce carbohydrates, carbs are not an essential macronutrient for most people.

The method of transitioning to a ketogenic diet is different for each individual person. Some people do well going cold turkey and jumping right into a strict keto diet, while others need to gradually reduce their carbohydrate intake a few weeks prior to starting a ketogenic diet to be able to succeed.

WHAT IS KETOSIS?

Ketosis is the state of having elevated blood ketone levels, meaning that your body is now effectively burning fat for energy instead of carbohydrates. This can happen a few different ways:

- By following a very low-carb, high-fat diet
- By fasting (not eating or consuming drinks with calories)
- By prolonged strenuous exercise

When you are in ketosis, your body produces ketones to use as fuel either from the fat you eat or from the stored fat in your body. When you're in a state of nutritional ketosis, it's easier to tap into stored fat for fuel than when on a carbohydrate-based diet. This is because your blood sugar level isn't constantly being spiked due to carbohydrate intake, which leads to reduced hunger pangs and cravings. Because fat is so satiating, it's easier to eat at a caloric deficit and not feel deprived.

When your body is already running on fat for fuel, it will more readily tap into stored fat. This is because insulin isn't constantly being secreted, so fat-burning mode is left on. When eating at a caloric deficit while following a ketogenic diet, weight loss occurs. A big benefit of a ketogenic diet for weight loss is that you preserve more lean body mass and lose a higher percentage of fat than on a carbohydrate-based diet. Limiting carbohydrate intake forces your body to run on fat as your primary fuel source and puts you into a state of nutritional ketosis.

WHAT ARE MACRONUTRIENTS?

Macronutrients include carbohydrates, protein, and fats. They're called *macronutrients* because they're typically consumed in large quantities and are measured in grams instead of micrograms or milligrams. Fat and protein are needed in large amounts to ensure that your body runs efficiently and to preserve lean body mass. Previously, carbohydrates were thought to be required, but now we know that isn't the case for most people because of gluconeogenesis. All of the foods that you eat contain at least one macronutrient. Carbohydrates and protein contain 4 calories (kcals) per gram, while fat contains 9 calories (kcals) per gram. On a typical ketogenic diet, the macronutrient breakdown is as follows:

- 60–75 percent of calories from fat
- 15–30 percent of calories from protein
- 5–10 percent of calories from carbohydrates

SIGNS YOU'RE IN KETOSIS

During the first two weeks of being on the keto diet, you may experience some symptoms that people refer to as the "keto flu." These symptoms may consist of the following:

- Headaches
- Chills
- Ashy skin tone
- Sensitivity to light and sound
- Nausea
- Dizziness
- Brain fog
- Insomnia
- Irritability
- GI issues

Some people say that the keto flu is your body's way of telling you that you're going through carbohydrate withdrawal, and in a way it is. These symptoms pass once your body adjusts to running on ketones, which can take anywhere from three days to two weeks.

There are a few things you can do to mitigate the symptoms of keto flu, or pass through them more quickly:

- Get plenty of electrolytes, in the form of bone broth, pickle juice, and so on
- Drink lots of water
- Make sure to get enough sleep
- If your doctor approves it, take magnesium and potassium supplements

Be patient with yourself—the brain fog will eventually go away, and your productivity will increase. After you've gone through the keto flu period, the good stuff starts. Positive signs that you're in ketosis include:

- Increased energy
- Increased focus
- Decreased appetite
- Improved mood
- Decreased inflammation
- Weight loss (if eating at a caloric deficit)
- Elevated blood ketone levels (beta-hydroxybutyrate [BHB])

Tools to Test for Ketones (in Breath, Urine, and Blood)

To be successful on the keto diet, you don't need to test yourself unless you're using this diet for therapeutic purposes or a doctor recommends it. For those who do want a measurement, there are a few ways to test whether you're in a state of nutritional ketosis, and some are more accurate than others. When you first start a keto diet, you may not want to invest over $100 for a blood or breath meter, so you may opt for ketone urine test strips. These urine test strips are very inexpensive (under $10 for one hundred strips) and test for the presence of ketone bodies, specifically the ketone acetoacetate. These strips are an indicator that your body is producing ketones and excreting them through urine. This is the first sign you're on your way to becoming fat-adapted, which means your body is using fatty acids and ketones as a primary fuel source, which is the point of a ketogenic diet.

Once you have been following a keto diet for a while and are committed, you may decide to purchase a blood glucose meter and blood ketone meter. These meters measure blood levels of the ketone beta-hydroxybutyrate (BHB), along with blood glucose. The level of ketones in your blood indicates how deep a level of ketosis you're in. Ketones and glucose have an inverse relationship, meaning when ketone levels rise, blood sugar lowers. Some diseases or conditions that are treated with a ketogenic diet may require deeper states of ketosis to be therapeutic. The higher ketone levels are, the deeper the state of nutritional ketosis. Blood meters cost $50 to $100 and are available online. We use the Keto-Mojo meter because at this time it's a fraction of the cost per strip of other brands. This meter is available on the *Keto-Mojo* website (https://keto-mojo .com) and other online retailers.

Those with a little more money to spend opt for a breath ketone meter. A couple of popular brands are Ketonix and LEVL. The Ketonix meter costs $150 to $250 and is available for purchase on www.ketonix.com. The LEVL meter is only available through the company's website (https:// levlnow.com) for a monthly fee, which starts at $99 per month. These meters measure the amount of acetone in the breath, which is formed from the breakdown of acetoacetate, indicating that you're burning fat. (However, this doesn't necessarily mean that you're in ketosis. For example, after an intense workout, your breath would show the presence of acetone because you're using fat for fuel during the workout, although you may not be in ketosis.)

TIPS FOR YOUR KETO JOURNEY

Because the keto diet can be tricky and very different from the standard American diet (SAD), here are a few tips to help you succeed:

- Don't steer clear of neighborhood picnics, potlucks, or barbecues! Use this book as a tool so you don't have to miss out on summertime fun. Make your own sauces and bring a side dish so you can easily enjoy a ketogenic meal at a barbecue.
- Eat a variety of foods, focusing on low-carb, high-fat options such as grass-fed meat and dairy; free-range chicken and eggs; wild-caught seafood; seeds and nuts; low-carb fruits, such as berries, avocados, coconuts, and olives; and low-carb vegetables, such as leafy greens, cruciferous vegetables, and other nonstarchy vegetables.
- Choose top-quality healthy fats, such as grass-fed lard or tallow, coconut oil, avocado oil, olive oil, and grass-fed butter and/or ghee.
- Eat foods high in magnesium and potassium, or take supplements to make sure you're getting enough electrolytes to avoid muscle cramping. Similarly, make sure you're getting 3–5 grams of sodium per day (or follow your physician's advice on sodium intake) to keep your electrolyte levels balanced. We recommend using a high-quality sea salt like Redmond Real Salt, which is typically available online or in many grocery stores. Some people choose to use an electrolyte powder, such as Dr. Berg's Electrolyte Powder or Vega Sport Hydrator.

- Stay hydrated—water is the best way to do this! A good formula for water consumption is (your body weight in pounds) × .5 = (number of ounces of water to consume). For example, a 150-pound person would need to consume a minimum of 150 × .5 = 75 fluid ounces per day.
- Get into a routine where you're meal planning and meal prepping to save time and money, and also to avoid having to resort to high-carb or fast food on busy days.

WHEN KETO BARBECUE RECIPES WILL COME IN HANDY

Picture this: You're thrilled to go to a neighbor's house for a cookout, or a friend's house for a potluck, or a family member's house for a birthday party. But you have absolutely no idea what you'll be able to eat! Or imagine you get the most serious barbecue craving of your life, and your favorite barbecue joint down the road is calling your name. What do you do?

This book is a must-have for any and all barbecue lovers. These recipes will save you time and time again from splurging on regular barbecue food that's full of hidden sugar, high-fructose corn syrup, and unhealthy fats. We might be a little bit biased, but these barbecue sauces are better than anything you'll find on the market. We took everyone's favorite sweet and tangy barbecue sauce—you know the one we're talking about—and made it even better while making it keto-friendly! You can make these sauces at a fraction of the price of what a store-bought keto barbecue sauce costs, and the flavors suit anyone's tastes. We also share a few different dry rubs, brines, and marinades that are so yummy that everyone will be asking you for the recipes. And we're grilling up a huge variety of meats, so there's something for even the pickiest eaters.

Whether you're hosting your own barbecue or you're attending one as a guest, there are a ton of reasons you'll want to whip up a keto recipe from this barbecue cookbook. Take out the stress of wondering if there'll be anything you can eat the next time you head to a party!

KETO BARBECUE BASICS

Flavorful meats and sauces are the key ingredients to a successful barbecue. Unfortunately, they're also usually minefields for people on a ketogenic diet. The secrets to juicy, tender, flavorful meat are dry rubs, brines, and marinades—and for even more flavor, barbecue sauces and condiments are the way to go! All these barbecue staples are easier than you think to make keto-friendly, and most also keep well so they can be made ahead of time.

Typical dry rubs are made with cornstarch and/or sugar, which can quickly add up to a lot of carbs. The dry rubs in this book are made with easy-to-find ingredients that pack a punch of flavor without all the sugar and carbs. In fact, they taste so good, you won't miss their carby counterparts at all.

The barbecue sauces in this book are sweetened with keto-friendly sweeteners, and they're developed to prevent crystallization. These recipes were tested with several keto sweeteners, including stevia, erythritol, monk fruit, and allulose. In our tests, allulose was the clear winner in terms of taste and texture. It has no bitter aftertaste or cooling effect, and it doesn't crystallize once cooled. However, if you use a different keto sweetener and your sauce crystallizes, reheating the sauce is a quick fix to dissolve the crystals.

Other barbecue basics include side dishes, salads, drinks, and desserts—and you'll find recipes for all of those here too! You'll find some reinvented classics, like Cauliflower "Potato" Salad (see Chapter 11), Pimento Cheese (see Chapter 5), and Creamy Cucumber Salad (see Chapter 11). Drinks are covered in Chapter 13 to give you inspiration (try the Mermaid Lemonade—it's a crowd-pleaser). And last but not least (because who would refuse dessert?), Chapter 14 features delicacies like Banana Cream Pie Bars; Red, White, and Blue Berry Parfaits; and Raspberry Crisp. These recipes focus on real foods, making them the perfect accompaniments to a great grilled dish.

KETO BARBECUE SAUCE INGREDIENT STAPLES

Even though keto barbecue sauces have a sweet heat and tangy flavor profile, the ingredients are quite different from regular barbecue sauce recipes. However, they're still easy to find (usually in your regular grocery store), and most can be stored in your pantry.

If you plan on making keto barbecue sauce regularly, it's helpful to keep the following on hand:

- Granulated, crystallized, or powdered allulose
- Tomato paste
- Various vinegars, such as apple cider and white wine
- Liquid smoke
- Salt
- Black pepper
- Onion powder
- Garlic powder
- Cayenne pepper or hot sauce

BARBECUE WITHOUT THE CARBS

Knowing what isn't hiding a ton of sugar or carbs at a barbecue can be a challenge, especially when you're at a potluck where everyone brought a dish to pass! Fortunately, the recipes in this book will provide you with low-carb, great-tasting recipes to easily whip up and bring to your next barbecue. Even the non–keto eaters will enjoy them, and there's no need to skimp on the condiments!

The goal of this book is to teach you how to make fabulous keto barbecue dishes so that you can enjoy the keto lifestyle without feeling deprived. These recipes will help you stay on track with your keto goals and provide you with the tools and knowledge to do so.

CHAPTER 2

DRY RUBS

MONTREAL DRY RUB

This seasoning blend is the base for a lot of the dry rub recipes in this cookbook and pairs well with just about any type of meat. Montreal Dry Rub packs a punch of flavor with a hint of heat. To reduce the spice level, simply scale back on the crushed red pepper flakes as desired. To add a smoky flavor, add up to 2 tablespoons smoked paprika.

Yields 1 cup

2 tablespoons coarse kosher salt

2 tablespoons crushed black peppercorns

2 tablespoons crushed coriander seeds

2 tablespoons crushed dill seeds

2 tablespoons granulated onion

2 tablespoons granulated garlic

2 tablespoons ground sweet paprika

2 tablespoons crushed red pepper flakes

1 In a medium bowl, whisk together all ingredients.

2 Store in a covered glass jar in the pantry up to 6 months.

Per Serving (Serving size: 1 teaspoon)
Calories: 5 | Fat: 0g | Protein: 0g | Sodium: 195mg | Fiber: 0g | Carbohydrates: 1g | Net Carbs: 1g | Sugar: 0g

BROWN SUGAR DRY RUB

This rub combines the savory flavor of our Montreal Dry Rub with the sweetness of brown sugar. The more keto-friendly Swerve brown sugar replacement used in this recipe is easy to find in many grocery stores or online.

Yields 1 cup

½ cup Swerve brown sugar replacement

½ cup Montreal Dry Rub (see recipe in this chapter)

1 In a medium bowl, whisk together all ingredients.

2 Store in a covered glass jar in the pantry up to 6 months.

Per Serving (Serving size: 1 teaspoon)
Calories: 2 | Fat: 0g | Protein: 0g | Sodium: 97mg | Fiber: 0g | Carbohydrates: 3g | Net Carbs: 1g | Sugar: 0g | Sugar Alcohol: 2g

COFFEE DRY RUB

Who says you need to drink a cup of joe to get your caffeine fix? This caffeinated rub combines the classic spices in our Montreal Dry Rub with coffee and brown "sugar" for a well-balanced seasoning blend that will take your meat to a whole new level.

Yields 1 cup

2 tablespoons Swerve brown sugar replacement

2 tablespoons finely ground medium- or dark-roast coffee

¾ cup Montreal Dry Rub (see recipe in this chapter)

1 In a medium bowl, whisk together all ingredients.

2 Store in a covered glass jar in the pantry up to 6 months.

Per Serving (Serving size: 1 teaspoon)
Calories: 4 | Fat: 0g | Protein: 0g | Sodium: 146mg | Fiber: 0g | Carbohydrates: 2g | Net Carbs: 1g | Sugar: 0g | Sugar Alcohol: 1g

---

CINNAMON DRY RUB

Don't knock this unusual dry rub until you try it— sweet cinnamon and brown "sugar" marry perfectly with our Montreal Dry Rub! Use this rub for everything from chicken and ribs to steaks and roasts.

Yields 1 cup

2 tablespoons Swerve brown sugar replacement

2 tablespoons ground cinnamon

¾ cup Montreal Dry Rub (see recipe in this chapter)

1 In a medium bowl, whisk together all ingredients.

2 Store in a covered glass jar in the pantry up to 6 months.

Per Serving (Serving size: 1 teaspoon)
Calories: 5 | Fat: 0g | Protein: 0g | Sodium: 146mg | Fiber: 1g | Carbohydrates: 2g | Net Carbs: 0g | Sugar: 0g | Sugar Alcohol: 1g

SOUTHWEST DRY RUB

This is a great go-to dry rub when you're in the mood for southwestern flavors! Use it on pork, beef, or chicken. Our favorite is to season boneless, skinless chicken breasts or thighs with this rub, grill them, and serve them up with fajita-style vegetables topped with sour cream.

Yields 1 cup

2 tablespoons coarse kosher salt

2 tablespoons ground black pepper

2 tablespoons ground cumin

2 tablespoons granulated onion

2 tablespoons granulated garlic

2 tablespoons ground sweet paprika

2 tablespoons dried Mexican oregano

1 tablespoon ancho chili powder

1 tablespoon chipotle chili powder

1 In a medium bowl, whisk together all ingredients.

2 Store in a covered glass jar in the pantry up to 6 months.

Per Serving
(Serving size: 1 teaspoon)
Calories: 6 | Fat: 0g | Protein: 0g | Sodium: 205mg | Fiber: 1g | Carbohydrates: 1g | Net Carbs: 0g | Sugar: 0g

What Is Mexican Oregano?

Mexican oregano is a different cultivar from the Mediterranean varieties of oregano. Mexican oregano is less minty and more peppery and citrusy in flavor. If you can't find Mexican oregano, you can substitute dried marjoram.

MEMPHIS DRY RUB

Memphis barbecue has a unique taste you'll definitely want to try! Ginger and rosemary give this dry rub its distinctive flavor.

Yields ¾ cup

2 tablespoons Swerve brown sugar replacement
1 tablespoon ground ginger
1 tablespoon dried rosemary
½ cup Montreal Dry Rub (see recipe in this chapter)

1 In a medium bowl, whisk together all ingredients.

2 Store in a covered glass jar in the pantry up to 6 months.

Per Serving (Serving size: 1 teaspoon)
Calories: 4 | Fat: 0g | Protein: 0g | Sodium: 130mg | Fiber: 0g | Carbohydrates: 2g | Net Carbs: 1g | Sugar: 0g | Sugar Alcohol: 1g

---

SMOKY PAPRIKA DRY RUB

Smoked paprika adds great depth of flavor to this dry rub. You can use a sweet or hot smoked paprika (or a mixture of both), based on your preference.

Yields 1 cup

2 tablespoons Swerve brown sugar replacement
2 tablespoons ground smoked paprika
¾ cup Montreal Dry Rub (see recipe in this chapter)

1 In a medium bowl, whisk together all ingredients.

2 Store in a covered glass jar in the pantry up to 6 months.

Per Serving (Serving size: 1 teaspoon)
Calories: 5 | Fat: 0g | Protein: 0g | Sodium: 147mg | Fiber: 0g | Carbohydrates: 2g | Net Carbs: 1g | Sugar: 0g | Sugar Alcohol: 1g

CHAPTER 3

BRINES AND MARINADES

BASIC BRINE

The purpose of a brine is to infuse the meat with salt water, which seasons the meat and yields a juicier result. Meat needs to be brined for at least 12 hours, but up to 24 hours is fine. If desired, feel free to add fresh herbs (like rosemary, thyme, sage, and so on) and aromatics (like onion, garlic, ginger, and so on) to your brine to play with the flavor profile.

Enough brine for 1 pound of meat

4 tablespoons coarse kosher salt
½ cup hot water
3½ cups cold water

1 In a large bowl, stir salt and hot water together until salt is dissolved.

2 Stir in cold water.

3 *To use:* Add 1 pound of meat, making sure meat is submerged in brine. Refrigerate covered 12 hours or up to 2 days before cooking meat.

Per Serving (about 4 servings)
Calories: 0 | Fat: 0g | Protein: 0g | Sodium: 5,760mg | Fiber: 0g | Carbohydrates: 0g | Net Carbs: 0g | Sugar: 0g

---

COKE ZERO MARINADE

If you enjoy the flavor of teriyaki, you're going to love this Coke Zero Marinade! Use it on beef, pork, or chicken.

Enough marinade for 1 pound of meat

½ cup Coke Zero
2 tablespoons tamari sauce
½ tablespoon Worcestershire sauce
1 medium clove garlic, peeled and crushed
¼ teaspoon ground black pepper

1 In a medium bowl, stir together all ingredients and then pour into a large zip-top plastic bag.

2 *To use:* Add 1 pound of meat, squeeze the air out of the bag, and seal the bag. Refrigerate 12 hours or up to 2 days before cooking meat.

Per Serving (about 4 servings)
Calories: 8 | Fat: 0g | Protein: 1g | Sodium: 523mg | Fiber: 0g | Carbohydrates: 1g | Net Carbs: 1g | Sugar: 0g

BUFFALO CHICKEN MARINADE

If you love buffalo chicken, this is the marinade for you! You can use it on bone-in or boneless chicken wings, thighs, or breasts.

Enough marinade for 1 pound of chicken

¼ cup Frank's RedHot Original sauce
2 tablespoons avocado oil
2 tablespoons fresh lime juice
2 medium cloves garlic, peeled and crushed
½ teaspoon salt

1 In a medium bowl, stir together all ingredients and then pour into a large zip-top plastic bag.

2 *To use:* Add 1 pound of chicken, squeeze the air out of the bag, and seal the bag. Refrigerate 12 hours or up to 2 days before cooking chicken.

Per Serving (about 4 servings)
Calories: 65 | Fat: 7g | Protein: 0g | Sodium: 750mg | Fiber: 0g | Carbohydrates: 1g | Net Carbs: 1g | Sugar: 0g

ASIAN MARINADE

This sweet, salty, and savory Asian-style marinade packs a punch of flavor—without the carbs! You can also reserve the marinade and boil it 3 minutes to use as a glaze after the meat is cooked.

Enough marinade for 1 pound of meat

3 tablespoons tamari sauce
2 tablespoons rice vinegar
1 tablespoon Swerve brown sugar replacement
2 medium cloves garlic, peeled and crushed
1 tablespoon grated fresh ginger
¼ teaspoon ground black pepper

1 In a medium bowl, stir together all ingredients and then pour into a large zip-top plastic bag.

2 *To use:* Add 1 pound of meat, squeeze the air out of the bag, and seal the bag. Refrigerate 12 hours or up to 2 days before cooking meat.

Per Serving (about 4 servings)
Calories: 12 | Fat: 0g | Protein: 2g | Sodium: 754mg | Fiber: 0g | Carbohydrates: 5g | Net Carbs: 3g | Sugar: 0g | Sugar Alcohol: 2g

ORANGE-CITRUS MARINADE

(pictured)

This marinade gives a wink and a nod to Faith and Lara's home state—sunny Florida! We love this marinade on chicken, and it's also great on pork. If you want to use it on fish, don't let it marinate longer than 30 minutes.

Enough marinade for 1 pound of meat

4 tablespoons fresh lemon juice

2 tablespoons avocado oil

2 tablespoons water

2 medium cloves garlic, peeled and crushed

1 tablespoon minced fresh rosemary

½ teaspoon salt

¼ teaspoon ground black pepper

1½ tablespoons fresh orange zest

1 In a medium bowl, stir together all ingredients and then pour into a large zip-top plastic bag.

2 *To use:* Add 1 pound of meat, squeeze the air out of the bag, and seal the bag. Refrigerate 12 hours or up to 2 days before cooking meat.

Per Serving (about 4 servings)

Calories: 74 | Fat: 7g | Protein: 0g | Sodium: 291mg | Fiber: 0g | Carbohydrates: 3g | Net Carbs: 3g | Sugar: 0g

---

GARLIC AND HERB MARINADE

This is sure to become your go-to marinade when you have meat in the refrigerator and you aren't sure how to flavor it. You'll be surprised at how these simple ingredients come together for a truly special result. Use one of the herbs mentioned here or a combination!

Enough marinade for 1 pound of meat

4 tablespoons fresh lemon juice

2 tablespoons avocado oil

2 tablespoons water

2 medium cloves garlic, peeled and crushed

1 tablespoon minced fresh thyme, rosemary, or oregano, or a combination

½ teaspoon salt

¼ teaspoon ground black pepper

1 In a medium bowl, stir together all ingredients and then pour into a large zip-top plastic bag.

2 *To use:* Add 1 pound of meat, squeeze the air out of the bag, and seal the bag. Refrigerate 12 hours or up to 2 days before cooking meat.

Per Serving (about 4 servings)

Calories: 67 | Fat: 7g | Protein: 0g | Sodium: 290mg | Fiber: 0g | Carbohydrates: 2g | Net Carbs: 2g | Sugar: 0g

LEMON-THYME MARINADE

The fresh, citrusy ingredients in this marinade will brighten up any meal! This marinade is perfect for chicken or pork. You can also use it on fish, but don't let it marinate more than 30 minutes.

Enough marinade for 1 pound of meat

4 tablespoons fresh lemon juice
2 tablespoons avocado oil
2 tablespoons water
1 medium clove garlic, peeled and crushed
1 tablespoon minced fresh thyme
½ teaspoon salt
¼ teaspoon ground black pepper
1½ tablespoons fresh lemon zest

1 In a medium bowl, stir together all ingredients and then pour into a large zip-top plastic bag.

2 *To use:* Add 1 pound of meat, squeeze the air out of the bag, and seal the bag. Refrigerate 12 hours or up to 2 days before cooking meat.

Per Serving (about 4 servings)
Calories: 67 | Fat: 7g | Protein: 0g | Sodium: 290mg | Fiber: 0g | Carbohydrates: 2g | Net Carbs: 2g | Sugar: 0g

---

BALSAMIC MARINADE

There's some kind of magic that happens when you use a really great-quality balsamic vinegar to flavor meat! Balsamic is a little on the high side when it comes to carbs, so the serving size is small. You don't need a lot for a ton of flavor.

Enough marinade for 1 pound of meat

3 tablespoons balsamic vinegar
2 tablespoons avocado oil
2 tablespoons water
2 medium cloves garlic, peeled and crushed
1 tablespoon minced fresh thyme, rosemary, or oregano, or a combination
½ teaspoon salt
¼ teaspoon ground black pepper
3 drops liquid stevia

1 In a medium bowl, stir together all ingredients and then pour into a large zip-top plastic bag.

2 *To use:* Add 1 pound of meat, squeeze the air out of the bag, and seal the bag. Refrigerate 12 hours or up to 2 days before cooking meat.

Per Serving (about 4 servings)
Calories: 75 | Fat: 7g | Protein: 0g | Sodium: 293mg | Fiber: 0g | Carbohydrates: 3g | Net Carbs: 3g | Sugar: 2g

CHAPTER 4

BARBECUE SAUCES AND GLAZES

SMOKY BOURBON BARBECUE SAUCE

With a smoky complexity and a hint of bourbon, this barbecue sauce is one for adult tastes. Two-thirds of the bourbon is cooked down with the sweetener, and the last tablespoon of bourbon is added at the end so the flavor isn't lost. If you'd like a smoky, maple-flavored bourbon sauce, add ¼ teaspoon ground fenugreek at the same time as the other spices.

Yields 1 cup

½ cup granulated (or crystallized) allulose sweetener
½ cup water
¼ cup white wine vinegar
¼ cup tomato paste
3 tablespoons bourbon, divided
½ tablespoon Dijon mustard
¾ teaspoon liquid smoke
½ teaspoon onion powder
½ teaspoon garlic powder
¼ teaspoon salt
⅛ teaspoon ground black pepper
⅛ teaspoon cayenne pepper

Per Serving
(Serving size: 2 tablespoons)
Calories: 22 | Fat: 0g |
Protein: 0g | Sodium: 161mg |
Fiber: 0g | Carbohydrates: 14g |
Net Carbs: 2g | Sugar: 13g

1 In a medium saucepan over medium heat, add allulose and water. Bring to a full boil.

2 Whisk in all remaining ingredients except 1 tablespoon bourbon and return to a full boil.

3 Boil 3–5 minutes, whisking frequently, until sauce reaches the desired thickness.

4 Whisk in remaining 1 tablespoon bourbon.

5 Serve immediately or store covered in a glass container in the refrigerator up to 1 month.

CLASSIC BARBECUE SAUCE

A little sweet, a little tart, a little spicy, a little smoky... our Classic Barbecue Sauce has it all, except all the unnecessary sugar! It's great on just about anything you want to grill up!

Yields ¾ cup

½ cup granulated (or crystallized) allulose sweetener

½ cup water

¼ cup tomato paste

¼ cup apple cider vinegar

½ tablespoon yellow mustard

1 teaspoon liquid smoke

1 teaspoon molasses

½ teaspoon onion powder

½ teaspoon garlic powder

¼ teaspoon ground smoked paprika

¼ teaspoon salt

¼ teaspoon ground black pepper

⅛ teaspoon cayenne pepper

Per Serving
(Serving size: 2 tablespoons)
Calories: 20 | Fat: 0g |
Protein: 1g | Sodium: 198mg |
Fiber: 1g | Carbohydrates: 20g |
Net Carbs: 4g | Sugar: 18g

1 In a medium saucepan over medium heat, add allulose and water. Bring to a full boil.

2 Whisk in all remaining ingredients and return to a full boil.

3 Boil 3–5 minutes, whisking frequently, until sauce reaches the desired thickness.

4 Serve immediately or store covered in a glass container in the refrigerator up to 1 month.

Can You Use Another Type of Keto Sweetener?

The barbecue sauce recipes in this book were tested with a few different sweeteners. Allulose yielded the best result by far in terms of flavor and texture.

SOUTH CAROLINA MUSTARD BBQ SAUCE

This South Carolina–style sauce packs a punch of mustard flavor, but it's balanced with both sweet and savory flavors. Whip up this sauce to make the best ham or pulled pork sandwiches of your life!

Yields 1½ cups

¾ cup yellow mustard
½ cup granulated (or crystallized) allulose sweetener
½ cup apple cider vinegar
2 tablespoons tomato paste
1 teaspoon Worcestershire sauce
1 teaspoon garlic powder
½ teaspoon molasses
½ teaspoon hot sauce
¼ teaspoon salt

1 In a medium saucepan over medium heat, add mustard and allulose. Bring to a full boil.

2 Whisk in all remaining ingredients and return to a full boil.

3 Boil 3–5 minutes, whisking frequently, until sauce reaches the desired thickness.

4 Serve immediately or store covered in a glass container in the refrigerator up to 1 month.

Per Serving (Serving size: 2 tablespoons)
Calories: 17 | Fat: 1g | Protein: 1g | Sodium: 252mg | Fiber: 1g | Carbohydrates: 10g | Net Carbs: 2g | Sugar: 9g

---

WHITE BARBECUE SAUCE

This Alabama-style, mayonnaise-based sauce is different from any barbecue sauce you've ever seen! You can use it as a dipping sauce for ribs, chicken, or pulled pork. It even makes a delicious keto salad dressing!

Yields 3 cups

2 cups full-fat mayonnaise
1 cup apple cider vinegar
1½ tablespoons Worcestershire sauce
1 medium clove garlic, peeled and crushed
1 tablespoon salt
1 tablespoon ground black pepper
½ teaspoon cayenne pepper

1 In a medium bowl, whisk together all ingredients.

2 Serve immediately or store covered in a glass container in the refrigerator up to 14 days.

Per Serving (Serving size: 2 tablespoons)
Calories: 128 | Fat: 13g | Protein: 0g | Sodium: 417mg | Fiber: 0g | Carbohydrates: 1g | Net Carbs: 1g | Sugar: 0g

PEACH-CHIPOTLE BARBECUE SAUCE

Sweet peach is the perfect foil for smoky, spicy chipotle powder! You'll notice this sauce is sweet and fruity when you first taste it before the heat builds on the back of your palate. It's so delightfully sweet, guests will never know it's keto-friendly.

Yields 1 cup

½ cup granulated (or crystallized) allulose sweetener

½ cup water

¼ cup white wine vinegar

2 tablespoons tomato paste

1 teaspoon onion powder

¼ teaspoon molasses

¼ teaspoon salt

⅛ teaspoon ground black pepper

⅛ teaspoon chipotle chili powder

⅓ cup sliced frozen peaches

Per Serving
(Serving size: 2 tablespoons)
Calories: 11 | Fat: 0g |
Protein: 0g | Sodium: 105mg |
Fiber: 0g | Carbohydrates: 14g |
Net Carbs: 2g | Sugar: 13g

1 In a medium saucepan over medium heat, add allulose and water. Bring to a full boil.

2 Whisk in all remaining ingredients and return to a full boil.

3 Boil 3–5 minutes, whisking frequently, until sauce reaches the desired thickness.

4 Remove from heat and cool slightly. Using an immersion or standing blender, puree until smooth.

5 Serve immediately or store covered in a glass container in the refrigerator up to 1 month.

Is Molasses Keto?

The molasses in this recipe adds a subtly sweet and smoky depth of flavor. The amount of carbs in ¼ teaspoon molasses (the amount used in this recipe) is 1.25g carbohydrates, which makes the per-serving carb number very keto-friendly.

HAWAIIAN BARBECUE SAUCE

The closest thing this barbecue sauce with ginger, tamari sauce, and pineapple compares to is a Hawaiian-style teriyaki. You won't believe this sweet sauce is keto—but it is! It's delicious with just about any meat, or use it as a dipping sauce for roasted cauliflower.

Yields 1 cup

½ cup granulated (or crystallized) allulose sweetener

½ cup water

¼ cup apple cider vinegar

⅓ cup chopped fresh pineapple

2 tablespoons tamari sauce

2 tablespoons tomato paste

1 medium clove garlic, peeled and minced

1 teaspoon grated fresh ginger

¼ teaspoon molasses

⅛ teaspoon salt

⅛ teaspoon ground black pepper

Per Serving
(Serving size: 2 tablespoons)
Calories: 17 | Fat: 0g |
Protein: 1g | Sodium: 319mg |
Fiber: 0g | Carbohydrates: 15g |
Net Carbs: 3g | Sugar: 14g

1 In a medium saucepan over medium heat, add allulose and water. Bring to a full boil.

2 Whisk in all remaining ingredients and return to a full boil.

3 Boil 3–5 minutes, whisking frequently, until sauce reaches the desired thickness.

4 Remove from heat and cool slightly. Using an immersion or standing blender, puree until smooth.

5 Serve immediately or store covered in a glass container in the refrigerator up to 1 month.

But Pineapple Isn't Keto

When you're following a ketogenic diet and lifestyle, it's important to remember that no foods are necessarily "off-limits." Instead, the amount of carbs correlates with the amount of food you eat, which is why portion control is important. This recipe uses ⅓ cup pineapple, which is divided among eight servings, and adds less than 1g net carbohydrates to each serving.

PIEDMONT VINEGAR BARBECUE SAUCE

One of the best things about barbecue sauces is how they differ by region across the US. Piedmont style is a more vinegary sauce than others. It's tangy and delicious with two types of vinegar, but it still has a balanced flavor profile and is low in carbs.

Yields 1 cup

½ cup granulated (or crystallized) allulose sweetener

6 tablespoons water

¼ cup tomato paste

¼ cup apple cider vinegar

2 tablespoons white wine vinegar

½ teaspoon molasses

½ teaspoon crushed red pepper flakes

½ teaspoon onion powder

½ teaspoon garlic powder

¼ teaspoon salt

⅛ teaspoon ground black pepper

Per Serving
(Serving size: 2 tablespoons)
Calories: 14 | Fat: 0g |
Protein: 0g | Sodium: 138mg |
Fiber: 0g | Carbohydrates: 14g |
Net Carbs: 2g | Sugar: 14g

1 In a medium saucepan over medium heat, add allulose and water. Bring to a full boil.

2 Whisk in all remaining ingredients and return to a full boil.

3 Boil 3–5 minutes, whisking frequently, until sauce reaches the desired thickness.

4 Serve immediately or store covered in a glass container in the refrigerator up to 1 month.

Can You Use Just One Kind of Vinegar for This Recipe?

If you want to use a single vinegar rather than two different types in this recipe, 6 tablespoons apple cider vinegar is recommended.

KANSAS CITY BARBECUE SAUCE

The distinguishing ingredient in Kansas City Barbecue Sauce is the chili powder! Chili powder is a spice blend made of paprika, ancho chili powder, cumin, cayenne pepper, garlic powder, onion powder, and Mexican oregano.

Yields 1 cup

½ cup granulated (or crystallized) allulose sweetener
½ cup water
¼ cup apple cider vinegar
¼ cup tomato paste
1 tablespoon yellow mustard
½ tablespoon chili powder
1 teaspoon molasses
¾ teaspoon onion powder
¼ teaspoon salt
¼ teaspoon garlic powder
⅛ teaspoon cayenne pepper
⅛ teaspoon ground black pepper

Per Serving
(Serving size: 2 tablespoons)
Calories: 17 | Fat: 0g |
Protein: 1g | Sodium: 174mg |
Fiber: 1g | Carbohydrates: 15g |
Net Carbs: 2g | Sugar: 14g

1 In a medium saucepan over medium heat, add allulose and water. Bring to a full boil.

2 Whisk in all remaining ingredients and return to a full boil.

3 Boil 3–5 minutes, whisking frequently, until sauce reaches the desired thickness.

4 Serve immediately or store covered in a glass container in the refrigerator up to 1 month.

DIET DR PEPPER GLAZE

You'll be surprised at just how many different ways you find to use this glaze. It's delicious for beef, chicken, and pork, but surprisingly, our favorite way to use it is on salmon! Don't skip the cloves here; just a little goes a long way, and it's the secret ingredient!

Yields ½ cup

¼ cup granulated (or crystallized) allulose sweetener

1 cup Diet Dr Pepper

2 tablespoons tamari sauce

1 tablespoon white wine vinegar

1 tablespoon tomato paste

½ teaspoon molasses

½ teaspoon hot sauce

¼ teaspoon garlic powder

¼ teaspoon onion powder

¼ teaspoon salt

⅛ teaspoon ground black pepper

1/16 teaspoon ground cloves

Per Serving
(Serving size: 2 teaspoons)
Calories: 5 | Fat: 0g |
Protein: 0g | Sodium: 232mg |
Fiber: 0g | Carbohydrates: 5g |
Net Carbs: 1g | Sugar: 4g

1. In a medium saucepan over medium heat, add all ingredients.

2. Bring to a boil and let boil about 8 minutes until thickened, whisking occasionally.

3. Serve immediately or store covered in a glass container in the refrigerator up to 1 month.

BALSAMIC GLAZE

Because balsamic vinegar is relatively high in carbohydrates, the serving size for Balsamic Glaze is only 1 teaspoon. It's delicious on pork or leafy greens salads.

Yields ¼ cup

½ cup balsamic vinegar

3 tablespoons granulated (or crystallized) allulose sweetener

⅛ teaspoon salt

Per Serving
(Serving size: 1 teaspoon)
Calories: 10 | Fat: 0g | Protein: 0g |
Sodium: 26mg | Fiber: 0g |
Carbohydrates: 5g | Net Carbs: 2g |
Sugar: 5g

1 In a medium saucepan over medium heat, add all ingredients.

2 Bring to a boil and cook about 5 minutes until reduced by about half, whisking occasionally.

3 Serve immediately or store covered in a glass container in the refrigerator up to 1 month.

RED WINE REDUCTION

This Red Wine Reduction doesn't get thick and syrupy like a standard reduction. Instead, it concentrates the flavor of wine into a thin, velvety sauce. We love serving it on grilled steak or chicken.

Yields ½ cup

1 cup dry red wine

1 cup beef stock

½ teaspoon dried Italian seasoning

½ teaspoon Swerve brown sugar replacement

¼ teaspoon onion powder

¼ teaspoon salt

⅛ teaspoon ground black pepper

1 tablespoon unsalted butter

1 In a medium saucepan over medium heat, add wine, beef stock, Italian seasoning, brown sugar replacement, onion powder, salt, and pepper.

2 Bring to a boil and let boil 20–25 minutes until reduced to about ¾ cup, whisking occasionally.

3 Strain reduction through a fine-mesh sieve; discard solids. Whisk in butter.

4 Serve immediately or store covered in a glass container in the refrigerator up to 2 weeks.

Per Serving (Serving size: 1 tablespoon)
Calories: 22 | Fat: 1g | Protein: 1g | Sodium: 132mg | Fiber: 0g |
Carbohydrates: 1g | Net Carbs: 1g | Sugar: 0g

CHAPTER 5

CONDIMENTS

HONEY MUSTARD

After you make this recipe once, you'll never want the store-bought stuff again! This sauce is low in carbs and very easy to whip up! Honey Mustard is perfect for dipping grilled chicken or slathering on a pulled pork sandwich.

Yields about ½ cup plus 2 tablespoons

½ cup full-fat mayonnaise
10 drops liquid stevia
1 tablespoon apple cider vinegar
½ tablespoon Dijon mustard
½ tablespoon yellow mustard
½ teaspoon onion powder
⅛ teaspoon ground sweet paprika
1/16 teaspoon salt

1 In a medium bowl, whisk together all ingredients until well combined.

2 Serve immediately or store covered in the refrigerator up to 5 days.

Per Serving (Serving size: 2 tablespoons)
Calories: 86 | Fat: 9g | Protein: 0g | Sodium: 123mg | Fiber: 0g | Carbohydrates: 0g | Net Carbs: 0g | Sugar: 0g

---

CLASSIC KETCHUP

It seems that every picnic, potluck, or barbecue features ketchup. Once you realize how easy it is to make ketchup at home, you may want to play around with the flavor profile and add other spices.

Yields 1 cup

½ cup granulated (or crystallized) allulose sweetener
½ cup water
¼ cup white wine vinegar
¼ cup tomato paste
½ tablespoon Dijon mustard
½ teaspoon onion powder
½ teaspoon garlic powder
¼ teaspoon salt
⅛ teaspoon ground black pepper

1 In a medium saucepan over medium heat, add allulose and water. Bring to a full boil.

2 Whisk in all remaining ingredients and return to a full boil.

3 Boil 3–5 minutes, stirring occasionally, until ketchup reaches the desired consistency.

4 Serve immediately or store covered in the refrigerator up to 1 month.

Per Serving (Serving size: 2 tablespoons)
Calories: 14 | Fat: 0g | Protein: 0g | Sodium: 306mg | Fiber: 0g | Carbohydrates: 14g | Net Carbs: 2g | Sugar: 13g

SPICY KETCHUP

Spicy Ketchup will become your new all-purpose condiment on everything from burgers to hot dogs to eggs.

Yields 1 cup

½ cup granulated (or crystallized) allulose sweetener
½ cup water
¼ cup white wine vinegar
¼ cup tomato paste
½ tablespoon Dijon mustard
½ teaspoon onion powder
½ teaspoon garlic powder
½ teaspoon cayenne pepper
¼ teaspoon salt
⅛ teaspoon ground black pepper

1 In a medium saucepan over medium heat, add allulose and water. Bring to a full boil.

2 Whisk in all remaining ingredients and return to a full boil.

3 Boil 3–5 minutes, stirring occasionally, until ketchup reaches the desired consistency.

4 Serve immediately or store covered in the refrigerator up to 1 month.

Per Serving (Serving size: 2 tablespoons)
Calories: 14 | Fat: 0g | Protein: 1g | Sodium: 161mg | Fiber: 0g | Carbohydrates: 14g | Net Carbs: 2g | Sugar: 13g

---

CAESAR DRESSING

Homemade keto Caesar Dressing is so much tastier than store-bought! This pairs well with grilled chicken and grilled vegetables; if you haven't tried grilled romaine lettuce, this dressing will make you want to!

Yields 1 cup

½ cup full-fat mayonnaise
¼ cup freshly grated Parmesan cheese
2 tablespoons water
1 tablespoon fresh lemon juice
½ teaspoon anchovy paste
½ teaspoon tamari sauce
½ teaspoon Dijon mustard
1 medium clove garlic, peeled and crushed

1 In a medium bowl, whisk together all ingredients until well combined.

2 Serve immediately or store covered in the refrigerator 3–5 days.

Per Serving (Serving size: 2 tablespoons)
Calories: 108 | Fat: 11g | Protein: 1g | Sodium: 191mg | Fiber: 0g | Carbohydrates: 1g | Net Carbs: 1g | Sugar: 0g

CARAMELIZED ONIONS

Caramelized Onions take burgers, steaks, and grilled chicken to the next level. The thyme is optional, but it adds a bright pop of flavor.

Serves 6

1 tablespoon extra-virgin olive oil

½ tablespoon unsalted butter

1 medium yellow onion, peeled, quartered, and thinly sliced

2 teaspoons minced fresh thyme leaves

¼ teaspoon salt

⅛ teaspoon ground black pepper

1 In a medium skillet over medium heat, heat oil and butter.

2 Add onion and cook about 15–20 minutes until deep caramel in color, stirring occasionally. Add a splash of water or turn the heat down a little at any time if the onion or the pan starts to get too dark.

3 Add thyme, salt, and pepper during the last 5 minutes of cooking, stirring occasionally.

4 Serve or store covered in the refrigerator up to 5 days.

Per Serving

Calories: 37 | Fat: 3g | Protein: 0g | Sodium: 97mg | Fiber: 1g | Carbohydrates: 2g | Net Carbs: 1g | Sugar: 1g

SMOKY GUACAMOLE

The smoky flavor in this guacamole comes in the form of chipotle chili powder and smoked paprika. If you like, you can use liquid smoke instead.

Serves 6

2 medium Hass avocados, peeled and pitted

2 tablespoons fresh lime juice

2 medium cloves garlic, peeled and crushed

¼ teaspoon chipotle chili powder

¼ teaspoon ground smoked paprika

¼ teaspoon coarse kosher salt

In a medium bowl, mash together all ingredients. Serve immediately.

Per Serving

Calories: 78 | Fat: 6g | Protein: 1g | Sodium: 103mg | Fiber: 3g | Carbohydrates: 5g | Net Carbs: 2g | Sugar: 0g

GREEN GODDESS DRESSING

(pictured)

This gorgeous green dressing is said to have been invented in San Francisco in the 1920s as a tribute to the play The Green Goddess. *With mayonnaise and sour cream as the base ingredients, it's completely keto-friendly! If you can't find tarragon, you can substitute 1 tablespoon minced fresh basil.*

Yields about 1 cup

½ cup full-fat mayonnaise

2 tablespoons full-fat sour cream

2 tablespoons water

3 tablespoons minced fresh parsley

2 tablespoons minced fresh chives

1 tablespoon minced fresh tarragon

1½ tablespoons fresh lemon juice

½ teaspoon anchovy paste

1 medium clove garlic, peeled and crushed

1 In a medium bowl, whisk together all ingredients until well combined.

2 Serve immediately or store covered in the refrigerator up to 5 days.

Per Serving (Serving size: 2 tablespoons)
Calories: 102 | Fat: 11g | Protein: 0g | Sodium: 109mg | Fiber: 0g | Carbohydrates: 1g | Net Carbs: 1g | Sugar: 0g

---

CHIMICHURRI SAUCE

This bold-flavored Argentinian condiment is perfect on just about anything that goes on the grill, including steak, pork, chicken, and even fish.

Yields about 1 cup

¾ cup tightly packed fresh Italian parsley

¾ cup tightly packed fresh cilantro

2 tablespoons chopped fresh oregano

2 medium cloves garlic, peeled

½ cup extra-virgin olive oil

3 tablespoons red wine vinegar

2 tablespoons fresh lime juice

½ teaspoon salt

½ teaspoon crushed red pepper flakes

1 To a blender or food processor, add all ingredients and process until a chunky paste forms.

2 Serve immediately or store covered in the refrigerator up to 2 days.

Per Serving (Serving size: 2 tablespoons)
Calories: 126 | Fat: 13g | Protein: 0g | Sodium: 149mg | Fiber: 1g | Carbohydrates: 2g | Net Carbs: 1g | Sugar: 0g

RANCH

Is it dip? Is it dressing? Is it sauce?! Yes, yes, and yes! In only 5 minutes you'll make the best keto Ranch of your life. To make this more like a dip, reduce the heavy whipping cream to ¼ cup and add ¼ cup full-fat sour cream.

Yields about 1 cup

½ cup full-fat mayonnaise
½ cup heavy whipping cream
2 tablespoons minced fresh parsley
1½ teaspoons minced fresh dill
½ teaspoon onion powder
½ teaspoon garlic powder
¼ teaspoon salt
⅛ teaspoon ground black pepper

1 In a medium bowl, whisk together all ingredients until well combined.

2 Serve immediately or store covered in the refrigerator up to 5 days.

Per Serving (Serving size: 2 tablespoons)
Calories: 146 | Fat: 15g | Protein: 1g | Sodium: 166mg | Fiber: 0g | Carbohydrates: 1g | Net Carbs: 1g | Sugar: 1g

TEX-MEX RANCH

Salsa, a little hot sauce, and a touch of cumin kick up the flavor of Ranch dressing, turning it into Tex-Mex Ranch. Use this to dress up tacos, fajitas, and salads, or for dipping grilled steak or chicken.

Yields about 1 cup plus 2 tablespoons

1 batch Ranch (see recipe in this chapter)
2 tablespoons salsa
½ teaspoon hot sauce
½ teaspoon ground cumin

1 In a medium bowl, whisk together all ingredients until well combined.

2 Serve immediately or store covered in the refrigerator up to 5 days.

Per Serving (Serving size: 2 tablespoons)
Calories: 131 | Fat: 14g | Protein: 0g | Sodium: 181mg | Fiber: 0g | Carbohydrates: 1g | Net Carbs: 1g | Sugar: 1g

BLUE CHEESE DRESSING

There's no way that Blue Cheese Dressing could be left out of a barbecue cookbook! Lusciously rich and creamy with savory flavor and blue cheese crumbles, this dressing just might make blue cheese converts out of the doubters in your family.

Yields 1 cup

⅓ cup full-fat mayonnaise
⅓ cup heavy whipping cream
⅓ cup crumbled blue cheese
1 teaspoon apple cider vinegar
½ teaspoon hot sauce
¼ teaspoon Worcestershire sauce
⅛ teaspoon salt
⅛ teaspoon ground black pepper
⅛ teaspoon garlic powder

1 In a medium bowl, whisk together all ingredients until well combined.

2 Serve or store covered in the refrigerator up to 5 days.

Per Serving (Serving size: 2 tablespoons)
Calories: 116 | Fat: 12g | Protein: 2g | Sodium: 173mg | Fiber: 0g | Carbohydrates: 1g | Net Carbs: 1g | Sugar: 0g

---

TZATZIKI SAUCE

A classic Greek condiment, this creamy sauce is garlicky, tangy, and herby—and now completely keto! You're going to love it on grilled chicken, beef, pork, or lamb! Or use it to top burgers or to dress salads.

Yields about 1 cup plus 2 tablespoons

6 tablespoons unsweetened plain whole milk Greek yogurt
6 tablespoons full-fat sour cream
1 tablespoon fresh lemon juice
1 tablespoon extra-virgin olive oil
2 teaspoons minced fresh dill
1 medium clove garlic, peeled and crushed
¼ teaspoon salt
⅛ teaspoon ground black pepper
¼ medium English cucumber, grated or finely diced
1 ounce feta cheese, crumbled

1 In a medium bowl, stir together all ingredients until well combined.

2 Serve or store covered in the refrigerator up to 5 days.

Per Serving (Serving size: 2 tablespoons)
Calories: 46 | Fat: 4g | Protein: 1g | Sodium: 100mg | Fiber: 0g | Carbohydrates: 1g | Net Carbs: 1g | Sugar: 1g

PICO DE GALLO
(pictured)

Mexican salsa fresca, also known as Pico de Gallo, is the best way to take a dish from ordinary to amazing. The bright flavor of cilantro perks up this whole recipe, but if cilantro isn't your thing, you can use flat-leaf parsley or a combination of flat-leaf parsley and fresh mint instead. If you can't find a serrano pepper, you can substitute a jalapeño.

Serves 10

2 cups cherry tomatoes, quartered

½ medium yellow onion, peeled and diced small

1 medium serrano pepper, seeded and minced

1 medium clove garlic, peeled and minced

½ cup chopped fresh cilantro

1½ tablespoons fresh lime juice

¼ teaspoon salt

1 In a large bowl, stir together all ingredients.

2 Serve immediately or store covered in the refrigerator up to 2 days.

Per Serving

Calories: 8 | Fat: 0g | Protein: 0g | Sodium: 60mg | Fiber: 1g | Carbohydrates: 2g | Net Carbs: 1g | Sugar: 1g

---

QUICK PICKLED ONIONS

Quick Pickled Onions is a deliciously dangerous recipe to have up your sleeve! You're going to find about a hundred ways to use them, including topping burgers, salads, and pulled meat of all kinds. And once you realize how easy they are to make, you're going to want to have a jar stashed in your refrigerator at all times.

Serves 32

2 cups thinly sliced red onion

1½ cups water

½ cup white wine vinegar

1 teaspoon salt

½ teaspoon whole black peppercorns

15 drops liquid stevia

1 In a 1-pint glass Mason jar, add all ingredients. Stir to combine. Cover the jar and refrigerate 8 hours.

2 Serve or store covered in the refrigerator up to 1 month.

Per Serving

Calories: 3 | Fat: 0g | Protein: 0g | Sodium: 7mg | Fiber: 0g | Carbohydrates: 1g | Net Carbs: 1g | Sugar: 0g

PIMENTO CHEESE

Pimento Cheese isn't just for serving on sandwiches! It also makes a killer burger or a great topping for grilled chicken or steak.

Serves 16

4 ounces full-fat cream cheese, at room temperature

⅔ cup full-fat mayonnaise

1 teaspoon white wine vinegar

1 teaspoon hot sauce

1 teaspoon Worcestershire sauce

½ teaspoon garlic powder

¼ teaspoon ground black pepper

4 ounces Monterey jack cheese, shredded

4 ounces Cheddar cheese, shredded

⅓ cup drained and diced jarred pimento

1 slice no-sugar-added bacon, cooked crispy and crumbled

1 medium scallion, trimmed and thinly sliced

Per Serving

Calories: 146 | Fat: 13g | Protein: 4g | Sodium: 197mg | Fiber: 0g | Carbohydrates: 1g | Net Carbs: 1g | Sugar: 1g

1 In a medium mixing bowl, beat together cream cheese, mayonnaise, vinegar, hot sauce, Worcestershire, garlic powder, and black pepper.

2 Stir in cheeses and pimento.

3 Top with crumbled bacon and scallion.

4 Serve immediately or store covered in the refrigerator up to 10 days.

CHAPTER 6

BARBECUE CHICKEN AND TURKEY

GRILLED CHICKEN LEG QUARTERS

This dish is great with any keto barbecue sauce on it. Simply brush 1 tablespoon sauce onto each leg quarter during the last 5 minutes of cooking.

Serves 4

4 (½-pound) chicken leg quarters
1 tablespoon avocado oil
1 teaspoon coarse kosher salt
¼ teaspoon ground black pepper

Per Serving

Calories: 505 | Fat: 24g |
Protein: 62g | Sodium: 834mg |
Fiber: 0g | Carbohydrates: 0g |
Net Carbs: 0g | Sugar: 0g

1 Lightly spray grill grate with cooking oil. Preheat grill to medium heat.

2 In a large bowl, add all ingredients and toss to coat.

3 Grill chicken about 45–60 minutes until skin is crispy and chicken has reached an internal temperature of 165°F and is fully cooked.

4 Let meat rest 5 minutes before serving.

GRILLED BONELESS CHICKEN THIGHS

There's just something about tender, juicy, flavorful dark meat! If you aren't sure if you like dark meat, go ahead and try boneless, skinless chicken thighs.

Serves 4

2 large (or 4 small) boneless, skinless chicken thighs (about 1½ pounds total weight)
2 tablespoons avocado oil
1 teaspoon coarse kosher salt
¼ teaspoon ground black pepper

Per Serving

Calories: 264 | Fat: 15g |
Protein: 28g | Sodium: 701mg |
Fiber: 0g | Carbohydrates: 0g |
Net Carbs: 0g | Sugar: 0g

1 Lightly spray grill grate with cooking oil. Preheat grill to medium heat.

2 In a large bowl, add all ingredients and toss to coat.

3 Grill chicken about 7–8 minutes per side until it has reached an internal temperature of 165°F and is fully cooked.

4 Let meat rest 5 minutes before serving.

GRILLED CHICKEN BREASTS

Chicken breasts are delicious when you use a brine or marinade, but if you're short on time, try this quick and easy method. Grill the chicken and add your favorite barbecue sauce to it too!

Serves 4

1 pound boneless, skinless chicken breasts
2 tablespoons avocado oil
1 teaspoon coarse kosher salt
¼ teaspoon ground black pepper

Per Serving
Calories: 185 | Fat: 9g |
Protein: 25g | Sodium: 623mg |
Fiber: 0g | Carbohydrates: 0g |
Net Carbs: 0g | Sugar: 0g

1 Lightly spray grill grate with cooking oil. Preheat grill to medium heat.

2 In a large bowl, add all ingredients and toss to coat.

3 Grill chicken about 7–8 minutes per side until it has reached an internal temperature of 165°F and is fully cooked.

4 Let meat rest 5 minutes before slicing across the grain and serving.

PULLED BARBECUE CHICKEN BREASTS

If you're grilling chicken breasts, throw a couple of extra ones on the grill to make Pulled Barbecue Chicken Breasts. We like to use ½ cup of barbecue sauce for 2–3 cups of pulled/shredded chicken. Feel free to swap out the Classic Barbecue Sauce in this recipe for your favorite sauce, but know that the nutrition information may change if you do.

Serves 4

1 batch Grilled Chicken Breasts (see recipe in this chapter), warmed
½ cup Classic Barbecue Sauce (see Chapter 4), warmed

Per Serving
Calories: 205 | Fat: 9g |
Protein: 26g | Sodium: 822mg |
Fiber: 1g | Carbohydrates: 20g |
Net Carbs: 3g | Sugar: 18g

1 In a large bowl, shred Grilled Chicken Breasts.

2 Add Classic Barbecue Sauce and toss to combine. Serve.

GRILLED CHICKEN WINGS

The beautiful thing about grilling chicken wings is that the skin gets crispy and the meat takes on a smoky flavor. In place of the salt and pepper, you can use your favorite dry rub to season the wings before cooking. Or go with a brine or marinade instead! The sky is the limit when it comes to flavoring chicken wings.

Serves 4

2 pounds chicken wings
1 tablespoon avocado oil
1 teaspoon coarse kosher salt
¼ teaspoon ground black pepper

Per Serving
Calories: 463 | Fat: 31g |
Protein: 40g | Sodium: 747mg |
Fiber: 0g | Carbohydrates: 0g |
Net Carbs: 0g | Sugar: 0g

1 Lightly spray grill grate with cooking oil. Preheat grill to medium or medium-high heat.

2 In a large bowl, add all ingredients and toss to coat.

3 Grill wings about 20–25 minutes until skin is crispy and chicken has reached an internal temperature of 165°F and is fully cooked. Serve.

How Many Chicken Wings Are in a Serving?

Two pounds of chicken wings is about ten drumettes (drums) and ten wingettes (flats). Each serving is about five total, with a mixture of drums and flats.

GUACAMOLE CHICKEN BURGERS

Take taco night in a new direction with these Guacamole Chicken Burgers! Skip the tortillas and serve them on keto Hamburger Buns (see Chapter 12) or on a bed of lettuce.

Serves 4

1 pound ground chicken

½ small yellow onion, peeled and grated

1 teaspoon salt

¼ teaspoon ground black pepper

4 tablespoons Smoky Guacamole (see Chapter 5)

4 tablespoons Pico de Gallo (see Chapter 5)

Per Serving
Calories: 201 | Fat: 11g | Protein: 22g | Sodium: 699mg | Fiber: 1g | Carbohydrates: 3g | Net Carbs: 2g | Sugar: 1g

1 In a large bowl, mix together chicken, onion, salt, and pepper.

2 Divide mixture into four portions and shape each into a patty.

3 *To Cook on the Stovetop:* Preheat a large (preferably cast-iron) skillet over medium-high to high heat. Once hot, add patties and turn heat down slightly to medium. Cook about 4–5 minutes per side until internal temperature is 165°F and patties are fully cooked.

4 *To Cook on a Grill:* Line grill grates with foil and lightly spray foil with avocado oil. Preheat grill to medium heat. Grill patties 5–6 minutes per side until internal temperature is 165°F and they are fully cooked.

5 *To Serve:* Top each cooked burger with 1 tablespoon Smoky Guacamole and 1 tablespoon Pico de Gallo.

Guacamole Tips

Normally we don't recommend making guacamole in advance because the avocado oxidizes pretty quickly and turns brown. It's still okay to eat, but it's not the prettiest thing! However, here's a tip that will keep your guacamole looking fresh for at least an hour: Put the guacamole in a bowl and layer a few lemon slices on top to cover most of the guacamole. Place a piece of plastic wrap directly on the lemon and put it in the refrigerator up to an hour before serving.

BARBECUE CHICKEN LETTUCE TACOS

Lettuce leaves act as the perfect low-carb taco "shells" for these Barbecue Chicken Lettuce Tacos! And to make them even more fun, set up a toppings bar with different keto-friendly toppings such as scallions, various cheeses, olives, and so on.

Serves 4

1 batch Pulled Barbecue Chicken Breasts (see recipe in this chapter), warmed
8 medium Bibb lettuce leaves
¼ cup shredded Cheddar cheese
2 tablespoons minced red onion
2 tablespoons full-fat sour cream

1 Divide Pulled Barbecue Chicken Breasts evenly among lettuce leaves.

2 Sprinkle Cheddar and onion on top. Add a dollop sour cream to each. Serve.

Per Serving
Calories: 249 | Fat: 12g | Protein: 28g | Sodium: 870mg | Fiber: 1g | Carbohydrates: 21g | Net Carbs: 4g | Sugar: 19g

---

BARBECUE CHICKEN AND PEPPER JACK SANDWICHES

Serve these sandwiches with a side of pickles and you'll feel like you're at your favorite barbecue restaurant! For messy barbecue sandwich lovers, it really doesn't get any better than this.

Serves 4

1 batch Pulled Barbecue Chicken Breasts (see recipe in this chapter), warmed
4 Hamburger Buns (see Chapter 12)
4 (1-ounce) slices pepper jack cheese

1 Divide chicken evenly among Hamburger Buns.

2 Place 1 slice cheese on top of each. Serve.

Per Serving
Calories: 548 | Fat: 35g | Protein: 43g | Sodium: 1,453mg | Fiber: 5g | Carbohydrates: 30g | Net Carbs: 9g | Sugar: 21g

INDIAN CHICKEN BURGERS

If you love Indian food, these burgers will become one of your favorite quick and easy ways to get your keto-friendly Indian food fix! Serve these burgers with a quick cucumber salad and cauliflower rice to make it a meal.

Serves 4

1 pound ground chicken
½ small yellow onion, peeled and grated
1 medium clove garlic, peeled and crushed
1 tablespoon fresh lemon juice
2 teaspoons garam masala
1 teaspoon salt
½ teaspoon ground cumin
¼ teaspoon ground black pepper

Per Serving
Calories: 180 | Fat: 9g |
Protein: 21g | Sodium: 651mg |
Fiber: 0g | Carbohydrates: 2g |
Net Carbs: 2g | Sugar: 0g

1 In a large bowl, mix together all ingredients.

2 Divide mixture into four portions and shape each into a patty.

3 *To Cook on the Stovetop:* Preheat a large (preferably cast-iron) skillet over medium-high to high heat. Add patties and turn heat down slightly to medium. Cook about 4–5 minutes per side until internal temperature is 165°F and patties are fully cooked. Serve.

4 *To Cook on a Grill:* Line grates with foil and lightly spray foil with avocado oil. Preheat grill to medium heat. Add patties and grill 5–6 minutes per side until internal temperature is 165°F and patties are fully cooked. Serve.

Can You Cook These on the Grates of a Grill?

The meat mixture for these burgers is fairly wet by design. That's how to get juicy, moist, and flavorful burgers! However, this means that the burgers will likely fall apart if you try to cook them directly on the grates of a grill.

SMOTHERED CHICKEN WITH HONEY MUSTARD

This dish is our keto copycat of Outback Steakhouse's Alice Spring Chicken. It's every bit as delicious as the original version, and we guarantee you won't even miss the carbs here! If you don't like honey mustard, feel free to use ¼ cup of your favorite barbecue sauce instead.

Serves 4

1 tablespoon unsalted butter

8 ounces button mushrooms, sliced

1 batch Grilled Chicken Breasts, sliced ¼" thick across the grain (see recipe in this chapter)

¼ cup Honey Mustard (see Chapter 5)

4 slices no-sugar-added bacon, cooked crispy and crumbled

2 ounces Monterey jack cheese, shredded

2 ounces Cheddar cheese, shredded

1 tablespoon minced chives

Per Serving

Calories: 429 | Fat: 29g |
Protein: 38g | Sodium: 1,057mg |
Fiber: 1g | Carbohydrates: 3g |
Net Carbs: 2g | Sugar: 1g

1 In a medium-large skillet over medium heat, heat butter. Add mushrooms and cook about 8 minutes until softened, stirring occasionally.

2 Preheat broiler. Line a baking sheet with foil.

3 Place sliced chicken on prepared baking sheet and top with Honey Mustard, cooked mushrooms, crumbled bacon, cheeses, and chives.

4 Broil until cheese is melted. Serve.

PULLED CHICKEN THIGHS

This recipe features tender, juicy dark-meat chicken thighs that are cooked until falling apart and paired with our Classic Barbecue Sauce from Chapter 4. Serve the meat in lettuce "tacos" or on keto Hamburger Buns (see Chapter 12).

Serves 8

2 pounds boneless, skinless chicken thighs

1 cup Classic Barbecue Sauce (see Chapter 4)

1 To a slow cooker, add all ingredients and cook on high 6–8 hours until chicken is tender, has an internal temperature of 165°F, and is fully cooked.

2 Cool slightly, then shred chicken with two forks. Serve warm.

Per Serving

Calories: 162 | Fat: 6g | Protein: 20g | Sodium: 282mg | Fiber: 1g | Carbohydrates: 20g | Net Carbs: 3g | Sugar: 18g

---

BARBECUE-RANCH CHICKEN SALAD

If you're looking for ideas on how to keep salad fresh and exciting, this is it! And to make this salad more attractive, you can arrange the toppings on this salad in pretty rows similar to a Cobb salad.

Serves 4

8 cups chopped romaine lettuce

1 batch Pulled Barbecue Chicken Breasts (see recipe in this chapter)

1 medium avocado, peeled, pitted, and thinly sliced

¼ medium English cucumber, thinly sliced

¼ cup halved cherry tomatoes

½ cup Ranch (see Chapter 5)

1 Divide lettuce evenly among four plates. Evenly divide chicken, avocado, cucumber, and tomatoes, and add on top of lettuce.

2 Drizzle on Ranch. Serve.

Per Serving

Calories: 428 | Fat: 29g | Protein: 28g | Sodium: 998mg | Fiber: 5g | Carbohydrates: 28g | Net Carbs: 7g | Sugar: 21g

GRILLED CHICKEN SHAWARMA KEBABS

Get ready for a culinary trip to the Middle East! If you want to simplify the ingredient list, instead of the cumin, coriander, black pepper, ginger, allspices, turmeric, fenugreek, cardamom, cloves, paprika, and cayenne pepper, just use 3 tablespoons of Lebanese Seven Spice.

Serves 4

3 tablespoons unsweetened plain whole milk yogurt

1 tablespoon fresh lemon juice

1 tablespoon extra-virgin olive oil

2 medium cloves garlic, peeled and crushed

¾ teaspoon salt

1 teaspoon ground cumin

1 teaspoon ground coriander

¼ teaspoon ground black pepper

¼ teaspoon ground ginger

¼ teaspoon ground allspice

¼ teaspoon ground turmeric

⅛ teaspoon ground fenugreek

⅛ teaspoon ground cardamom

⅛ teaspoon ground cloves

⅛ teaspoon ground sweet paprika

⅛ teaspoon cayenne pepper

1 pound boneless, skinless chicken breasts, cut into 1" cubes

1 In a large bowl, add all ingredients except chicken. Whisk to combine well, then add chicken. Use your hands to combine so chicken is well coated.

2 Cover and refrigerate at least 2 hours, but up to 1 day.

3 Lightly spray grill grate with cooking oil. Preheat grill to medium heat.

4 Skewer chicken on four metal or wooden skewers.

5 Grill kebabs about 4–7 minutes per side until chicken has reached an internal temperature of 165°F and is fully cooked.

6 Let meat rest 5 minutes before serving.

Per Serving
Calories: 168 | Fat: 6g | Protein: 26g | Sodium: 485mg | Fiber: 1g | Carbohydrates: 2g | Net Carbs: 1g | Sugar: 1g

Grilling Tip

If you're using wooden skewers, be sure to soak them in water for 20 minutes right before skewering the chicken so they don't burn or splinter in your meat.

THE BEST TURKEY BURGERS

If you usually go for beef burgers, give these turkey burgers a try! You'll be surprised at how flavorful they are. To let their flavor develop even more, mix up the meat mixture, shape it into patties, wrap with plastic wrap, and pop them in the refrigerator up to 4 hours before cooking.

Serves 4

1 pound ground turkey

½ small yellow onion, peeled and grated

1 teaspoon tamari sauce

1 teaspoon Worcestershire sauce

1 teaspoon liquid smoke

1 teaspoon apple cider vinegar

1 medium clove garlic, peeled and crushed

¾ teaspoon salt

¼ teaspoon ground black pepper

Per Serving

Calories: 194 | Fat: 9g |
Protein: 24g | Sodium: 325mg |
Fiber: 0g | Carbohydrates: 2g |
Net Carbs: 2g | Sugar: 1g

1 In a large bowl, mix together all ingredients.

2 Divide mixture into four portions and shape each into a patty.

3 *To Cook on the Stovetop:* Preheat a large (preferably cast-iron) skillet over medium-high to high heat. Once hot, add patties and turn heat down slightly to medium. Cook about 4–5 minutes per side until each patty has an internal temperature of 165°F and is fully cooked. Serve.

4 *To Cook on a Grill:* Line grill grates with foil and lightly spray foil with avocado oil. Preheat grill to medium heat. Add patties and grill 5–6 minutes per side until each patty has an internal temperature of 165°F and is fully cooked. Serve.

SOUTHWESTERN TURKEY BURGERS

(pictured)

The Tex-Mex flavors in these Southwestern Turkey Burgers are a great way to make your taco nights exciting! If you don't have time to make the Pico de Gallo from Chapter 5, feel free to use your favorite sugar-free salsa instead.

Serves 4

1 batch The Best Turkey Burgers (see recipe in this chapter), warmed

4 (1-ounce) slices pepper jack cheese

1 medium avocado, peeled, pitted, and thinly sliced

½ cup Pico de Gallo (see Chapter 5)

2 tablespoons chopped fresh cilantro

1 Place a cooked patty on each of four plates. Place a slice of cheese on top of each burger.

2 Evenly divide avocado, Pico de Gallo, and cilantro and top each burger. Serve.

Per Serving

Calories: 361 | Fat: 22g | Protein: 32g | Sodium: 535mg | Fiber: 3g | Carbohydrates: 6g | Net Carbs: 3g | Sugar: 2g

---

CHICKEN PARMESAN BURGERS

If you don't have time to make the Hamburger Buns, you can cook this dish like a gratin and serve it along with steamed cauliflower or broccoli to make it a full meal.

Serves 4

1 batch Grilled Chicken Breasts, sliced ¼" thick across the grain (see recipe in this chapter)

4 tablespoons sugar-free marinara sauce

½ cup shredded mozzarella cheese

4 teaspoons grated Parmesan cheese

4 Hamburger Buns (see Chapter 12)

1 Preheat broiler. Line a baking sheet with foil.

2 Place cooked chicken on prepared baking sheet and top with marinara, mozzarella, and Parmesan.

3 Broil until cheese is melted.

4 Divide cheesy chicken equally among Hamburger Buns. Serve.

Per Serving

Calories: 486 | Fat: 30g | Protein: 39g | Sodium: 1,270mg | Fiber: 4g | Carbohydrates: 12g | Net Carbs: 8g | Sugar: 3g

CHAPTER 7

BARBECUE PORK

GLAZED PORK TENDERLOIN

This Glazed Pork Tenderloin is moist and juicy. Serve with Loaded Mashed "Potatoes" and Bacon-Sautéed Green Beans (see Chapter 12 for recipes) for a full meal!

Serves 8

1 (3½-pound) pork tenderloin, silverskin membrane removed

1 teaspoon salt

½ teaspoon ground black pepper

¼ cup Balsamic Glaze (see Chapter 4), divided

Per Serving
(Serving size: ¹⁄₃ pound cooked)
Calories: 196 | Fat: 4g | Protein: 32g | Sodium: 709mg | Fiber: 0g | Carbohydrates: 7g | Net Carbs: 4g | Sugar: 7g

1. Preheat oven to 375°F.

2. Rub pork loin with salt and pepper and place fat side up on a rack in a baking pan.

3. Bake uncovered 1 hour.

4. Pour half Balsamic Glaze in a small dish and reserve for serving; use the other half to brush on pork loin.

5. Cook an additional 15–35 minutes until pork reaches an internal temperature of 145°F. Let meat rest 5 minutes. (Alternatively you can grill the pork until it reaches an internal temperature of 145°F.) Serve.

GRILLED PORK TENDERLOIN

This tenderloin pairs perfectly with Jalapeño-Cheddar "Corn Bread" (see Chapter 12) and Tomato-Cucumber Salad (see Chapter 11).

Serves 4

1 (1½-pound) pork tenderloin, silverskin membrane removed

2 tablespoons avocado oil

2 teaspoons Memphis Dry Rub (see Chapter 2)

Per Serving
(Serving size: ¹⁄₃ pound cooked)
Calories: 217 | Fat: 11g | Protein: 27g | Sodium: 357mg | Fiber: 0g | Carbohydrates: 1g | Net Carbs: 0g | Sugar: 0g

1. Lightly spray grill grate with cooking oil. Preheat grill to high heat.

2. Rub tenderloin with oil. Then cover pork with Memphis Dry Rub.

3. Add pork to grill and cook covered 1 minute on each side.

4. Reduce heat to low and grill an additional 8–10 minutes until internal temperature reaches 145°F.

5. Let meat rest at least 5 minutes before serving.

PORK RIBS

(pictured)

Delicious, fall-off-the-bone keto pork ribs—what could be better than that? These ribs are so sweet, tender, and flavorful, you'll have a hard time believing you can eat them and stay on track, but you can!

Serves 4

1 (2-pound) rack pork ribs, silverskin membrane removed

⅓ cup Brown Sugar Dry Rub (see Chapter 2)

¼ cup Classic Barbecue Sauce (see Chapter 4)

Per Serving

Calories: 581 | Fat: 37g | Protein: 54g | Sodium: 705mg | Fiber: 1g | Carbohydrates: 20g | Net Carbs: 4g | Sugar: 9g | Sugar Alcohol: 8g

1 Preheat oven to 275°F.

2 Place ribs in a large baking pan and coat ribs with Brown Sugar Dry Rub. Cover pan with foil.

3 Bake ribs covered 3–4 hours until ribs reach an internal temperature of 145°F. Remove foil and brush with Classic Barbecue Sauce.

4 Turn on broiler and broil uncovered 3–5 minutes until sauce starts to caramelize. Serve.

SHREDDED PORK BUTT

This pork butt cooked in a slow cooker is a ridiculously easy recipe to make. Flavor it with your favorite barbecue sauce, top it with Quick Pickled Onions (see Chapter 5), and serve it on Hamburger Buns (see Chapter 12).

Serves 10

1 (4-pound) pork butt

2 teaspoons salt

1 teaspoon ground black pepper

¼ cup water

Per Serving
(Serving size: ¹⁄₃ pound cooked)

Calories: 305 | Fat: 18g | Protein: 30g | Sodium: 640mg | Fiber: 0g | Carbohydrates: 0g | Net Carbs: 0g | Sugar: 0g

1 Add all ingredients to a slow cooker and cook on low 8 hours until internal temperature is 145°F.

2 Use two forks to shred pork. Serve with 2 tablespoons cooking liquid on top to keep meat moist.

GRILLED PORK CHOPS

Bring on summertime—these keto chops are perfect for a backyard barbecue. These Grilled Pork Chops are tender and juicy without the normal sugar and carbs that accompany other marinades and dry rubs!

Serves 4

1 batch Garlic and Herb Marinade (see Chapter 3)

2 (8-ounce) center-cut pork chops (at least 1" thick)

2 teaspoons Montreal Dry Rub (see Chapter 2)

Per Serving

Calories: 146 | Fat: 10g | Protein: 10g | Sodium: 403mg | Fiber: 0g | Carbohydrates: 2g | Net Carbs: 2g | Sugar: 0g

1 In a large zip-top bag, combine Garlic and Herb Marinade and pork chops. Marinate refrigerated at least 30 minutes or up to 1½ hours. Pat pork chops dry (do not wash off marinade).

2 Preheat gas or charcoal grill to medium-high.

3 Season chops with Montreal Dry Rub on both sides.

4 Turn burners down to medium on gas grill. Add chops and cook covered 3–4 minutes on each side.

5 Cook uncovered, flipping occasionally, another 4–5 minutes until internal temperature reaches at least 145°F. Time varies depending on thickness of pork chops and if bone-in or boneless.

6 Remove from heat. Let meat rest at least 5 minutes before serving.

SMOKED PORK SHOULDER

Smoked Pork Shoulder is perfect by itself, or you can shred it and make a pulled pork sandwich! A good rule for smoking pork is 60–90 minutes per pound. Serve this with your favorite keto barbecue sauce.

Serves 14

1 (5-pound) pork shoulder
¼ cup Brown Sugar Dry Rub (see Chapter 2)

Per Serving
(Serving size: ¹⁄₃ pound cooked)
Calories: 161 | Fat: 5g | Protein: 27g |
Sodium: 203mg | Fiber: 0g |
Carbohydrates: 2g | Net Carbs: 2g |
Sugar: 0g | Sugar Alcohol: 2g

1 Preheat smoker to 225°F–250°F.

2 Pat pork shoulder dry and score the fat side with a sharp knife. Season pork with Brown Sugar Dry Rub.

3 Place pork on smoker fat side up. Try to avoid any direct hot spots.

4 Close smoker and smoke pork 7½ hours until it reaches an internal temperature of at least 145°F.

5 Remove pork from smoker. Wrap in foil or butcher paper. Allow meat to rest at least 1 hour before serving.

PULLED PORK SANDWICHES

These Pulled Pork Sandwiches are super-versatile! Make them with your favorite keto barbecue sauce. If you'd like, you can also toast the buns.

Serves 4

1 pound Shredded Pork Butt (see recipe in this chapter), warmed
½ cup Classic Barbecue Sauce (see Chapter 4), warmed
4 Hamburger Buns (see Chapter 12)

1 In a medium bowl, combine Shredded Pork Butt and Classic Barbecue Sauce.

2 Evenly distribute pork among bottom halves of Hamburger Buns. Top with top halves of buns. Serve.

Per Serving
Calories: 448 | Fat: 32g |
Protein: 33g | Sodium: 1,143mg |
Fiber: 5g | Carbohydrates: 30g |
Net Carbs: 9g | Sugar: 20g

BANH MI–INSPIRED BURGERS

Give the traditional Vietnamese-French fusion sandwich a keto twist! If you'd like, substitute shredded pork or ground chicken for the ground pork.

Serves 4

1 pound ground pork
1 tablespoon Montreal Dry Rub (see Chapter 2)
4 Hamburger Buns (see Chapter 12), toasted
¼ cup Quick Pickled Onions (see Chapter 5)
¼ medium cucumber, thinly sliced
2 tablespoons thinly sliced carrots
1 medium radish, trimmed and thinly sliced
1 medium scallion, trimmed and thinly sliced
1 medium jalapeño pepper, seeded and sliced
¼ cup chopped fresh cilantro
2 lime wedges

Per Serving

Calories: 414 | Fat: 28g |
Protein: 24g | Sodium: 669mg |
Fiber: 5g | Carbohydrates: 14g |
Net Carbs: 9g | Sugar: 3g

1 In a medium bowl, add pork and Montreal Dry Rub. Mix until well combined.

2 Divide mixture into four portions and shape each into a patty.

3 *To Cook on the Stovetop:* Preheat a large (preferably cast-iron) skillet over medium-high heat. Add patties and turn heat down slightly to medium. Cook about 4–5 minutes per side until patties reach an internal temperature of 165°F and are fully cooked.

4 *To Cook on a Grill:* Line grill grates with aluminum foil and lightly spray foil with avocado oil. Preheat grill to medium heat. Grill patties 5–6 minutes per side until patties reach an internal temperature of 165°F and are fully cooked.

5 Place 1 burger on each bottom half of buns and top with sliced vegetables and cilantro. Squeeze lime wedges over burgers and top with top halves of buns. Serve.

BBQ PORK CABBAGE CUPS
(pictured)

These BBQ Pork Cabbage Cups take no time to whip up! They're perfect if you don't like to bake or don't have our keto buns on hand. Simply pile the delicious barbecue pork on top of the cabbage leaves for a quick meal.

Serves 4

1 pound Shredded Pork Butt (see recipe in this chapter), warmed

½ cup Smoky Bourbon Barbecue Sauce (see Chapter 4), warmed

8 large red or green cabbage leaves

1 medium scallion, trimmed and sliced

¼ cup chopped fresh cilantro

1 In a medium bowl, combine Shredded Pork Butt and Smoky Bourbon Barbecue Sauce.

2 Evenly divide pork mixture among cabbage leaves.

3 Top with sliced scallion and cilantro. Serve.

Per Serving

Calories: 267 | Fat: 14g | Protein: 24g | Sodium: 658mg | Fiber: 2g | Carbohydrates: 18g | Net Carbs: 4g | Sugar: 15g

---

PORK AND POBLANO SLIDERS

These sliders are a great way to impress your guests at your next backyard barbecue—they are supereasy to make and are the perfect finger food! Feel free to toast the slider rolls if you'd like.

Serves 4

1 pound Shredded Pork Butt (see recipe in this chapter), warmed

½ cup South Carolina Mustard BBQ Sauce (see Chapter 4), warmed

1 medium poblano pepper, seeded, grilled, and cut into 8 slices

8 Hamburger Buns (see Chapter 12)

¼ cup crumbled white cheese (queso fresco)

1 In a medium bowl, combine Shredded Pork Butt and South Carolina Mustard BBQ Sauce.

2 Place 1 slice pepper on bottom half of each Hamburger Bun.

3 Evenly distribute pork on top of pepper slices. Top with white cheese and top half of buns. Serve.

Per Serving

Calories: 756 | Fat: 51g | Protein: 46g | Sodium: 1,717mg | Fiber: 10g | Carbohydrates: 33g | Net Carbs: 15g | Sugar: 13g

CHAPTER 8

BARBECUE BEEF

SHREDDED BARBECUE BEEF

Shredded Barbecue Beef is an easy recipe that the entire family will love! Make a large batch in the pressure cooker or slow cooker for barbecues and potlucks. The secret ingredient in this dish is our amazing homemade Classic Barbecue Sauce.

Serves 8

1 (3-pound) chuck roast
2 tablespoons Montreal Dry Rub (see Chapter 2)
1 tablespoon avocado oil
1 cup water
1 cup Classic Barbecue Sauce (see Chapter 4), warmed

Per Serving
Calories: 298 | Fat: 9g |
Protein: 43g | Sodium: 413mg |
Fiber: 1g | Carbohydrates: 21g |
Net Carbs: 4g | Sugar: 18g

1 Pat roast dry with paper towel. Season on both sides with Montreal Dry Rub.

2 Turn pressure cooker to the "Sauté" function and add oil. Wait 2 minutes for pressure cooker to heat up, then add roast. Let it sear on one side, then turn it and sear on the other side, about 2 minutes per side.

3 Add water. Secure lid and close pressure release. Cook on High Pressure 60 minutes. Allow pressure cooker to naturally release pressure.

4 Drain water except for a few tablespoons. Shred beef with two forks, then add Classic Barbecue Sauce. Thoroughly incorporate sauce into shredded beef. Serve.

Make It in a Slow Cooker!

To make this in a slow cooker, simply omit the oil and water from the ingredients. Add the chuck roast to the slow cooker, sprinkle with Montreal Dry Rub, and top with Classic Barbecue Sauce. Cook on low 6–8 hours until it can be easily shredded. Shred the meat with two forks and stir the sauce into the meat. Cook an additional 20–30 minutes in the slow cooker until sauce is thickened.

GLAZED BEEF SHORT RIBS

These juicy and tender short ribs are supereasy to make on the grill in foil packets! Then they're slathered with barbecue sauce and finished off over direct heat. Feel free to substitute the Classic Barbecue Sauce called for in this recipe with your favorite keto sauce.

Serves 4

4 pounds beef short ribs, silverskin membrane removed

¼ cup Brown Sugar Dry Rub (see Chapter 2)

6 ice cubes

½ cup Classic Barbecue Sauce (see Chapter 4)

Per Serving

Calories: 921 | Fat: 51g | Protein: 108g | Sodium: 771mg | Fiber: 1g | Carbohydrates: 27g | Net Carbs: 4g | Sugar: 18g | Sugar Alcohol: 6g

1 Preheat grill to medium heat.

2 Thoroughly cover ribs with dry rub.

3 Tear off a 12" × 12" piece of foil. Place one-third of the ribs on the foil. Place 2 ice cubes on top of ribs. Cover ribs with a second piece of foil and seal the ends to make a packet.

4 Repeat with remaining ribs and ice cubes.

5 Place foil packets on grill, close grill, and cook 1½–2 hours until ribs are tender.

6 Remove ribs from foil packets. Brush with sauce. Return ribs to grill and cook covered another 5–10 minutes, flipping occasionally, until internal temperature is 145°F. Serve.

Can You Substitute Beef Back Ribs?

Yes! Beef back ribs may take a little less time to cook on the grill, so check them after 1¼ hours to see how tender they are.

SMOKED BRISKET

Smoked Brisket is perfect as is but is also delicious shredded in a keto brisket sandwich! This recipe is perfect whether you enjoy fatty or lean brisket, and the burnt ends are the best part.

Serves 20

1 (8-pound) beef brisket, fat trimmed and silverskin membrane removed

⅓ cup Brown Sugar Dry Rub (see Chapter 2)

Per Serving
(Serving size: ¹/₃ pound cooked)
Calories: 351 | Fat: 19g |
Protein: 36g | Sodium: 139mg |
Fiber: 0g | Carbohydrates: 2g |
Net Carbs: 0g | Sugar: 0g |
Sugar Alcohol: 2g

1 Preheat smoker to 225°F–250°F.

2 Pat brisket dry with paper towels. Trim silverskin from brisket. Season brisket with Brown Sugar Dry Rub.

3 Place brisket on smoker fat side up.

4 Close smoker and smoke brisket 7–8 hours until it reaches an internal temperature of 165°F.

5 Remove brisket and wrap in butcher paper. Return it to smoker and cook an additional 4–8 hours until the thickest part of the brisket reaches at least 200°F.

6 Let brisket rest at least 1 hour before serving.

How to Trim Brisket

The silverskin on the underside of the brisket, also known as sinew, is a thin membrane found on different types of meats. Beef ribs have them as well. It's best to remove this before smoking because it does not break down or tenderize when the brisket is smoked. To trim brisket, put the brisket fat side down and trim off any gray-colored meat. Cut off any large skin pieces from the brisket. Flip the brisket so the fatty side is facing up and trim the fat layer to ¼" thick.

GARLIC BUTTER RIB EYE

Juicy and tender, this rib eye is topped with a garlic butter that literally gets our mouths watering! If you have any leftovers, make good ol' steak and eggs the next morning! Serve with a sliced avocado and sprinkle with salt, pepper, and even some crushed red pepper flakes.

Serves 4

2 tablespoons salted butter, at room temperature

1 medium clove garlic, peeled and minced

1 teaspoon minced fresh parsley

2 (16-ounce) bone-in rib eyes

1 tablespoon avocado oil

2 teaspoons Montreal Dry Rub (see Chapter 2)

Per Serving

Calories: 488 | Fat: 28g | Protein: 55g | Sodium: 258mg | Fiber: 0g | Carbohydrates: 1g | Net Carbs: 1g | Sugar: 0g

1 In a small bowl, combine butter, garlic, and parsley. Mix well and refrigerate until ready to use.

2 Lightly spray grill grate with cooking oil. Preheat grill to medium-high heat and close cover. Once grill is up to temperature, turn off half of the burners.

3 Pat rib eyes dry with a paper towel and brush with oil. Sprinkle with Montreal Dry Rub.

4 Sear steaks on direct heat 2–3 minutes each side until grill marks are visible.

5 Move steaks to indirect heat (where the burners are not on) and cook covered 10–12 minutes until steaks reach an internal temperature of at least 130°F.

6 Remove steaks and top with garlic butter. Let meat rest 5 minutes before serving.

TERIYAKI-GRILLED SKIRT STEAK

Our tender skirt steak brings all the Asian flare without the carbs! It's perfect to slice up and add to a stir-fry served with cauliflower rice.

Serves 4

⅔ cup Asian Marinade (see Chapter 3)
1 (2-pound) skirt steak
1 teaspoon salt
1 medium scallion, trimmed and sliced

Per Serving

Calories: 396 | Fat: 19g |
Protein: 47g | Sodium: 2,050mg |
Fiber: 0g | Carbohydrates: 9g |
Net Carbs: 5g | Sugar: 1g |
Sugar Alcohol: 4g

1 In a gallon-sized zip-top bag or shallow pan, add Asian Marinade. Add steak and turn to coat thoroughly. Seal the bag or cover pan and marinate steak refrigerated at least 1 hour.

2 Lightly spray grill grate with cooking oil. Preheat grill to medium-high heat.

3 Sprinkle steak with salt. Grill 3–5 minutes on each side until desired doneness (about 140°F for medium or 160°F for well-done).

4 Let meat rest 10 minutes before slicing. Top with sliced scallion and serve.

What Part Is the Skirt Steak From?

Skirt steak is taken from the diaphragm of the cow, which is located between the chest and the abdomen. This is a lean cut of beef and can be tough if you don't marinate or tenderize it prior to cooking.

SMOTHERED NEW YORK STRIP STEAK

Tender and juicy, this Smothered New York Strip Steak is covered with tender mushrooms and onion and topped with Gorgonzola cheese. It's incredibly easy to make and is the perfect dinner to impress that special someone.

Serves 8

2 tablespoons unsalted butter

2 teaspoons Worcestershire sauce

½ large yellow onion, peeled and sliced

8 ounces baby bella mushrooms, sliced

1 medium clove garlic, peeled and minced

½ teaspoon salt

¼ teaspoon ground black pepper

4 (12-ounce) New York strip steaks

2 tablespoons Montreal Dry Rub (see Chapter 2)

2 ounces Gorgonzola cheese, crumbled

Per Serving

Calories: 460 | Fat: 27g | Protein: 40g | Sodium: 478mg | Fiber: 1g | Carbohydrates: 4g | Net Carbs: 3g | Sugar: 1g

1 Lightly spray grill grate with cooking oil. Preheat grill to medium-high heat.

2 In a large skillet over medium heat, melt butter. Add Worcestershire, onion, and mushrooms. Cook about 10 minutes until onion is translucent, stirring occasionally. Add garlic, salt, and pepper.

3 Cook 2 minutes, then remove from heat and cover.

4 Sprinkle steaks with Montreal Dry Rub. Grill steaks covered 5–6 minutes on each side for medium-rare or until desired doneness (about 140°F for medium or 160°F for well-done).

5 Remove steaks and let them rest 5 minutes. Top with Gorgonzola cheese and mushroom mixture. Serve.

Can You Substitute Blue Cheese?

You absolutely can substitute blue cheese for Gorgonzola cheese. If you don't have either, you can even use 1 tablespoon grass-fed butter!

SOUTHWESTERN GRILLED FLANK STEAK

This flank steak is supereasy to whip up and is perfect for low-carb fajitas! FYI: Flank steak can become tough when it's overcooked, so it's best cooked to medium-rare.

Serves 8

2 pounds flank steak
2 tablespoons Southwest Dry Rub (see Chapter 2)
¼ cup avocado oil
Juice of 1 medium lime
¼ cup chopped fresh cilantro

Per Serving
Calories: 484 | Fat: 39g | Protein: 25g | Sodium: 251mg | Fiber: 0g | Carbohydrates: 1g | Net Carbs: 1g | Sugar: 0g

1 In a gallon-sized zip-top bag, add all ingredients except cilantro. Seal the bag and marinate refrigerated at least 1 hour.

2 Lightly spray grill grate with cooking oil. Preheat grill to medium-high heat.

3 Grill steak 5–6 minutes on each side for medium-rare or until desired doneness (about 140°F for medium or 160°F for well-done).

4 Remove steak and top with cilantro. Let meat rest 10 minutes before serving.

GRILLED BEEF RIBS

These ribs make for a perfect outdoor meal for family get-togethers. Team them up with all the barbecue sides that you and your family enjoy.

Serves 4

1 (3½-pound) rack beef ribs, silverskin membrane removed
2 tablespoons Memphis Dry Rub (see Chapter 2)
½ cup Classic Barbecue Sauce (see Chapter 4)

Per Serving
Calories: 892 | Fat: 53g | Protein: 83g | Sodium: 590mg | Fiber: 1g | Carbohydrates: 22g | Net Carbs: 4g | Sugar: 18g | Sugar Alcohol: 1g

1 Lightly spray grill grate with cooking oil. Preheat grill to medium-low heat.

2 Season ribs with Memphis Dry Rub and add to grill. Make sure not to put ribs directly over flames.

3 Grill ribs covered 1½ hours and then top with Classic Barbecue Sauce. Cook covered an additional 10–15 minutes until sauce is caramelized and ribs reach an internal temperature of 145°F. Rest ribs 5 minutes and then serve.

CINNAMON-GRILLED SIRLOIN

This grilled sirloin is the perfect mixture of sweet and savory. It'll have your taste buds watering and your friends asking what the secret ingredient is!

Serves 4

2 (12-ounce) sirloin steaks
1 tablespoon avocado oil
1 tablespoon Cinnamon Dry Rub
(see Chapter 2)

Per Serving
Calories: 384 | Fat: 22g |
Protein: 37g | Sodium: 73mg |
Fiber: 0g | Carbohydrates: 1g |
Net Carbs: 1g | Sugar: 0g

1 Lightly spray grill grate with cooking oil. Preheat grill to medium-high heat.

2 Pat steaks dry with a paper towel. Brush steaks with oil, then season with Cinnamon Dry Rub.

3 Grill steaks 4–5 minutes on each side for medium-rare or until they reach desired doneness (about 140°F for medium or 160°F for well-done).

4 Let meat rest 10 minutes before serving.

BARBECUE BEEF–CHEDDAR SANDWICHES

Tender Shredded Barbecue Beef, savory Cheddar cheese, and red onion sandwiched in a keto hamburger bun—these sandwiches are the perfect keto barbecue dish!

Serves 4

4 Hamburger Buns
(see Chapter 12)
4 (1-ounce) slices Cheddar cheese
2 cups Shredded Barbecue Beef
(see recipe in this chapter)
4 thin slices red onion

Per Serving
Calories: 653 | Fat: 35g |
Protein: 60g | Sodium: 1,056mg |
Fiber: 5g | Carbohydrates: 32g |
Net Carbs: 11g | Sugar: 21g

1 Preheat oven to 400°F. Line a baking sheet with parchment paper or foil.

2 Place bottoms of Hamburger Buns on prepared baking sheet. Top each with 1 slice Cheddar and ½ cup Shredded Barbecue Beef. Place tops of buns on top of beef.

3 Cook 3–4 minutes until beef is warm and cheese is melted. Remove from oven and top each sandwich with a slice of red onion. Serve.

JALAPEÑO-CHEDDAR BURGERS

If you like your burgers to pack some heat, then this recipe is for you! These juicy burgers have diced jalapeños, so in every bite you'll get some spice. And if you like them extra spicy, feel free to top your burgers with even more sliced jalapeños. If you don't want to serve these burgers in buns, use one head of butter lettuce for lettuce-wrapped burgers.

Serves 4

1 pound 80/20 ground beef

2 medium jalapeño peppers, seeded and diced

½ teaspoon ground black pepper

½ teaspoon garlic powder

¼ teaspoon onion powder

¼ teaspoon salt

4 (1-ounce) slices Cheddar cheese

4 Hamburger Buns (see Chapter 12)

Per Serving

Calories: 567 | Fat: 38g | Protein: 37g | Sodium: 847mg | Fiber: 5g | Carbohydrates: 11g | Net Carbs: 6g | Sugar: 2g

1 Lightly spray grill grate with cooking oil. Preheat grill to medium heat.

2 In a medium bowl, combine ground beef, jalapeños, black pepper, garlic powder, onion powder, and salt. Knead together with your hands until well combined, then form mixture into four equally sized balls. Flatten them into patties and make a thumbprint in the middle of each to keep them from puffing up.

3 Grill burgers until cooked to your desired doneness, about 3–4 minutes per side for medium (aim for 145°F–160°F).

4 Remove burgers from grill and top each with 1 slice cheese. Serve on Hamburger Buns.

Don't Like Your Burgers Spicy?

To lessen the heat, add just one jalapeño to the burgers and make sure to remove the seeds. This will reduce the heat considerably.

THE BEST BURGERS

These burgers are perfect for an anytime meal—lunch or dinner. If you prefer not to serve these on buns, you can use one head of butter lettuce to make lettuce-wrapped burgers.

Serves 4

2 pounds 80/20 ground beef

2 teaspoons Worcestershire sauce

3 teaspoons ground smoked paprika

1 teaspoon ground black pepper

1 teaspoon garlic powder

½ teaspoon onion powder

½ teaspoon cayenne pepper

¼ teaspoon salt

4 (1-ounce) slices sharp American cheese

8 slices no-sugar-added bacon, cooked

1 medium avocado, peeled, pitted, and sliced

4 Hamburger Buns (see Chapter 12)

Per Serving

Calories: 909 | Fat: 58g | Protein: 65g | Sodium: 1,525mg | Fiber: 8g | Carbohydrates: 19g | Net Carbs: 11g | Sugar: 5g

1 Lightly spray grill grate with cooking oil. Preheat grill to medium heat.

2 In a medium bowl, combine beef, Worcestershire, paprika, black pepper, garlic powder, onion powder, and cayenne pepper.

3 Knead together with your hands until well combined, then form mixture into four equally sized balls. Flatten them into patties and make a thumbprint in the middle of each to keep them from puffing up.

4 Sprinkle with salt.

5 Grill burgers until cooked to your desired doneness, 4–5 minutes per side for medium (aim for 145°F–160°F). Remove burgers from grill and top with cheese, allowing it to melt from the residual heat.

6 Let burgers rest 5 minutes. Top with bacon and avocado slices. Serve on Hamburger Buns.

Stuff Them!

You can also stuff these burgers with cheese. Simply form meat into eight balls instead of four. Then flatten the balls into thin patties. In the middle of four of the patties place your favorite cheese. Then top with another patty. Press the edges together to seal the cheese inside.

BURGERS WITH PEPPER AND ONION

A juicy burger topped with perfectly cara-melized sautéed pepper and onion—what could be better? These burgers will have your mouth watering, and you'll be going back for seconds. If you don't want to use buns for these burgers, use one head of butter lettuce for lettuce-wrapped burgers.

Serves 4

½ tablespoon avocado oil

1 medium green bell pepper, seeded and sliced

1 medium yellow onion, peeled and sliced

¾ teaspoon ground black pepper, divided

¾ teaspoon garlic powder, divided

¼ teaspoon salt

1 pound 80/20 ground beef

¼ teaspoon onion powder

4 Hamburger Buns (see Chapter 12)

Per Serving

Calories: 473 | Fat: 30g |
Protein: 31g | Sodium: 666mg |
Fiber: 5g | Carbohydrates: 15g |
Net Carbs: 10g | Sugar: 4g

1 Heat a large skillet over medium heat. Add oil, bell pepper, and onion.

2 Sprinkle with ¼ teaspoon black pepper, ¼ teaspoon garlic powder, and salt. Stir well, making sure bell pepper and onion are coated completely with seasonings and oil. Sauté 10–15 minutes until bell pepper and onion are cara-melized, stirring occasionally. Remove from heat and set aside.

3 Lightly spray grill grate with cooking oil. Preheat grill to medium heat.

4 In a medium bowl, combine ground beef, remaining ½ teaspoon black pepper, remaining ½ teaspoon garlic pow-der, and onion powder. Knead together with your hands until well combined, then form mixture into four equally sized balls. Flatten them into patties and make a thumbprint in the middle of each to keep them from puffing up.

5 Grill burgers until cooked to your desired doneness, 3–4 minutes per side for medium (aim for 145°F–160°F).

6 Remove burgers from grill and let rest 4–5 minutes while you reheat bell pepper and onion on the stovetop.

7 Top burgers with caramelized bell pepper and onion. Serve on Hamburger Buns.

GREEK BURGERS WITH TZATZIKI

These tender burgers are studded with feta in every bite and topped with delicious tzatziki, cucumber, tomato, red onion, and arugula for a Greek spin on an American classic! If you don't want to serve them with buns, use one head of butter lettuce for lettuce-wrapped burgers.

Serves 4

1 pound 80/20 ground beef

2 ounces feta cheese, crumbled

½ teaspoon ground black pepper

¾ teaspoon garlic powder

½ teaspoon salt

1 teaspoon Italian seasoning

½ cup Tzatziki Sauce (see Chapter 5)

¼ medium English cucumber, thinly sliced

4 thin slices red onion

4 large thin slices tomato

1 cup arugula

4 Hamburger Buns (see Chapter 12)

Per Serving
Calories: 543 | Fat: 36g |
Protein: 35g | Sodium: 1,042mg |
Fiber: 5g | Carbohydrates: 14g |
Net Carbs: 9g | Sugar: 5g

1 Lightly spray grill grate with cooking oil. Preheat grill to medium heat.

2 In a medium bowl, combine ground beef, feta, pepper, garlic powder, salt, and Italian seasoning. Knead together with your hands until well combined, then form mixture into four equally sized balls. Flatten them into patties and make a thumbprint in the middle of each to keep them from puffing up.

3 Grill burgers until cooked to your desired doneness, 4–5 minutes per side for medium (aim for 145°F–160°F). Remove burgers from grill.

4 Let burgers rest 5 minutes, then top each with 2 tablespoons Tzatziki Sauce, sliced cucumber, onion, tomato, and arugula.

5 Serve on Hamburger Buns.

BLUE CHEESE BURGERS

We wanted to create a juicy steak topped with blue cheese and caramelized onions but in burger form... and voilà! If you don't like blue cheese, simply swap it out for feta, goat, or Gorgonzola crumbles. If you don't want to use buns for these burgers, use one head of butter lettuce for lettuce-wrapped burgers.

Serves 4

1 teaspoon avocado oil
1 medium yellow onion, peeled and sliced
¼ teaspoon salt
1 pound 80/20 ground beef
½ teaspoon ground black pepper
½ teaspoon garlic powder
¼ teaspoon onion powder
4 ounces blue cheese crumbles
4 Hamburger Buns (see Chapter 12)

Per Serving

Calories: 571 | Fat: 38g | Protein: 37g | Sodium: 990mg | Fiber: 5g | Carbohydrates: 14g | Net Carbs: 9g | Sugar: 3g

1 Heat a medium or large skillet over medium heat. Add oil, onion, and salt. Stir to combine, making sure onion is coated completely with salt and oil. Sauté 10–12 minutes until onion is caramelized, stirring occasionally. Remove from heat and set aside.

2 Lightly spray grill grate with cooking oil. Preheat grill to medium heat.

3 In a medium bowl, combine ground beef, pepper, garlic powder, and onion powder. Knead together with your hands until well combined, then form mixture into four equally sized balls. Flatten them into patties and make a thumbprint in the middle of each to keep them from puffing up.

4 Grill burgers until cooked to your desired doneness, 3–4 minutes per side for medium (aim for 145°F–160°F). Remove burgers from grill. Top each burger with 1 ounce blue cheese.

5 Let burgers rest 4–5 minutes while you reheat onion on the stovetop.

6 Top burgers with caramelized onion. Serve on Hamburger Buns.

BLT BURGERS

We love this burger spin on a traditional BLT. Juicy burgers plus crispy bacon, fresh tomato, and lettuce make these mouthwatering burgers irresistible.

Serves 4

1 pound 80/20 ground beef

½ teaspoon ground black pepper

½ teaspoon garlic powder

¼ teaspoon onion powder

½ teaspoon salt

4 tablespoons full-fat mayonnaise

4 Hamburger Buns (see Chapter 12)

8 slices no-sugar-added bacon, cooked

4 large thin slices tomato

4 lettuce leaves

Per Serving

Calories: 655 | Fat: 47g |
Protein: 39g | Sodium: 1,286mg |
Fiber: 5g | Carbohydrates: 12g |
Net Carbs: 7g | Sugar: 3g

1 Lightly spray grill grate with cooking oil. Preheat grill to medium heat.

2 In a medium bowl, combine ground beef, pepper, garlic powder, onion powder, and salt. Knead together with your hands until well combined, then form mixture into four equally sized balls. Flatten them into patties and make a thumbprint in the middle of each to keep them from puffing up.

3 Grill burgers until cooked to your desired doneness, 4–5 minutes per side for medium (aim for 145°F–160°F). Remove burgers from grill.

4 Let burgers rest 5 minutes. Spread mayonnaise on Hamburger Buns and add burgers. Top each burger with 2 slices bacon, 1 slice tomato, and 1 lettuce leaf. Serve.

THE WORKS BARBECUE BURGERS

Your taste buds will be watering over these juicy burgers topped with Cheddar cheese, crispy bacon, red onion, romaine lettuce, and sweet keto barbecue sauce. If you have another keto barbecue sauce you'd like to use, simply switch out the Classic Barbecue Sauce for your favorite.

Serves 4

1 pound 80/20 ground beef
½ teaspoon ground black pepper
½ teaspoon garlic powder
¼ teaspoon onion powder
½ teaspoon salt
4 (1-ounce) slices Cheddar cheese
4 Hamburger Buns
(see Chapter 12)
8 slices no-sugar-added bacon, cooked
4 thin red onion slices
4 romaine lettuce leaves
4 tablespoons Classic Barbecue Sauce (see Chapter 4), warmed

Per Serving
Calories: 687 | Fat: 45g |
Protein: 46g | Sodium: 1,480mg |
Fiber: 5g | Carbohydrates: 22g |
Net Carbs: 9g | Sugar: 12g

1 Lightly spray grill grate with cooking oil. Preheat grill to medium heat.

2 In a medium bowl, combine ground beef, pepper, garlic powder, onion powder, and salt. Knead together with your hands until well combined, then form mixture into four equally sized balls. Flatten them into patties and make a thumbprint in the middle of each to keep them from puffing up.

3 Grill burgers until cooked to your desired doneness, 4–5 minutes per side for medium (aim for 145°F–160°F). Remove burgers from grill.

4 Top each burger with 1 slice Cheddar cheese. Let rest 5 minutes and then place on Hamburger Buns. Top each with 2 slices bacon, 1 slice red onion, 1 lettuce leaf, and 1 tablespoon Classic Barbecue Sauce. Serve.

"MAC" AND CHEESE BURGERS

What can be better than a juicy burger? A juicy burger with some mac and cheese on it! These southern burgers stay low-carb by using homemade keto buns, our famous keto "mac" and cheese, and a perfectly seasoned burger—plus more Cheddar cheese, of course!

Serves 4

1 pound 80/20 ground beef
½ teaspoon ground black pepper
½ teaspoon garlic powder
¼ teaspoon onion powder
½ teaspoon salt
4 (1-ounce) slices Cheddar cheese
4 Hamburger Buns (see Chapter 12)
1 cup Cheddar Cauliflower "Mac" and Cheese (see Chapter 12), warmed

Per Serving

Calories: 781 | Fat: 54g |
Protein: 46g | Sodium: 1,315mg |
Fiber: 7g | Carbohydrates: 18g |
Net Carbs: 11g | Sugar: 5g

1 Lightly spray grill grate with cooking oil. Preheat grill to medium heat.

2 In a medium bowl, combine ground beef, pepper, garlic powder, onion powder, and salt. Knead together with your hands until well combined, then form mixture into four equally sized balls. Flatten them into patties and make a thumbprint in the middle of each to keep them from puffing up.

3 Grill burgers until cooked to your desired doneness, 4–5 minutes per side for medium (aim for 145°F–160°F). Remove burgers from grill.

4 Top each burger with 1 slice Cheddar cheese. Let burgers rest 5 minutes and then place on Hamburger Buns. Top each burger with ¼ cup Cheddar Cauliflower "Mac" and Cheese. Serve.

STUFFED CHEDDAR CHEESE BURGERS

These perfectly seasoned burgers ooze with Cheddar goodness. They're a fun keto spin on a traditional burger that everyone will love. If you'd like, top these burgers with keto ketchup, mayonnaise, mustard, and lettuce.

Serves 4

2 pounds 80/20 ground beef
½ teaspoon ground black pepper
½ teaspoon garlic powder
¼ teaspoon onion powder
½ teaspoon salt
4 ounces Cheddar cheese, shredded
4 Hamburger Buns (see Chapter 12)

Per Serving
Calories: 782 | Fat: 50g | Protein: 58g | Sodium: 1,053mg | Fiber: 4g | Carbohydrates: 11g | Net Carbs: 7g | Sugar: 2g

1 Lightly spray grill grate with cooking oil. Preheat grill to medium heat.

2 In a medium bowl, combine ground beef, pepper, garlic powder, onion powder, and salt. Knead together with your hands until well combined, then form mixture into eight equally sized balls. Flatten them into thin patties. Spoon equal amounts Cheddar cheese onto the center of four patties. Top each with another patty. Press edges together to seal cheese inside.

3 Grill burgers until cooked to your desired doneness, 4–5 minutes per side for medium (aim for 145°F–160°F). Remove burgers from grill.

4 Let rest 5 minutes, then serve on Hamburger Buns.

Don't Have Freshly Shredded Cheddar?

You can use bagged shredded cheese, but it won't melt as well. Or stuff burgers with a slice of cheese folded into a square.

PIMENTO CHEESEBURGERS

Pimento Cheese is a southern favorite that is amazing on burgers! These perfectly seasoned burgers are topped with Cheddar cheese and then piled high with Pimento Cheese.

Serves 4

1 pound 80/20 ground beef
½ teaspoon ground black pepper
½ teaspoon garlic powder
¼ teaspoon onion powder
½ teaspoon salt
4 (1-ounce) slices Cheddar cheese
4 Hamburger Buns (see Chapter 12)
1 cup Pimento Cheese
(see Chapter 5)

Per Serving
Calories: 858 | Fat: 64g |
Protein: 46g | Sodium: 1,388mg |
Fiber: 5g | Carbohydrates: 13g |
Net Carbs: 8g | Sugar: 3g

1 Lightly spray grill grate with cooking oil. Preheat grill to medium heat.

2 In a medium bowl, combine ground beef, pepper, garlic powder, onion powder, and salt. Knead together with your hands until well combined, then form mixture into four equally sized balls. Flatten them into patties and make a thumbprint in the middle of each to keep them from puffing up.

3 Grill burgers until cooked to your desired doneness, 4–5 minutes per side for medium (aim for 145°F–160°F). Remove burgers from grill.

4 Top each burger with 1 slice Cheddar cheese. Let rest 5 minutes, then place on bottom halves of Hamburger Buns. Top each burger with ¼ cup Pimento Cheese and top half of Hamburger Bun. Serve.

CHAPTER 9

SAUSAGES AND HOT DOGS

GRILLED KIELBASA

If you're in need of a superquick meal, then Grilled Kielbasa is where it's at! In the US, store-bought kielbasa is typically smoked and fully cooked, so you just need to heat it up. You can whip up this meal in less than 10 minutes and still stay on your diet!

Serves 4

1 pound cooked kielbasa
4 Hot Dog Buns (see Chapter 12)
1 cup sauerkraut
4 tablespoons yellow mustard

Per Serving
Calories: 634 | Fat: 51g |
Protein: 22g | Sodium: 1,520mg |
Fiber: 6g | Carbohydrates: 16g |
Net Carbs: 10g | Sugar: 5g

1 Lightly spray grill grate with cooking oil. Preheat grill to medium-high heat.

2 Slice kielbasa in half lengthwise and then widthwise so you have four pieces.

3 Grill kielbasa 5–6 minutes or until it starts to get charred and warm throughout.

4 Serve in Hot Dog Buns and top each with ¼ cup sauerkraut and 1 tablespoon mustard.

ATLANTA HOT DOGS

These Atlanta-style hot dogs are topped with Beanless Chili and Vinaigrette Coleslaw. Spicy meets tangy in this delicious duo.

Serves 4

4 (1.75-ounce) all-beef hot dogs
4 Hot Dog Buns (see Chapter 12)
1 cup Beanless Chili
(see Chapter 12)
1 cup Vinaigrette Coleslaw
(see Chapter 11)

Per Serving
Calories: 503 | Fat: 39g |
Protein: 18g | Sodium: 879mg |
Fiber: 5g | Carbohydrates: 15g |
Net Carbs: 10g | Sugar: 4g

1 Lightly spray grill grate with cooking oil. Preheat grill to medium heat.

2 Grill hot dogs 4–5 minutes until fully warmed. Place in Hot Dog Buns.

3 Top each hot dog with ¼ cup Beanless Chili and ¼ cup Vinaigrette Coleslaw. Serve.

ITALIAN SAUSAGE SANDWICHES

You'll love this grilled Italian sausage topped with tender pepper and onion, packaged deliciously in a keto hot dog bun with low-carb marinara and gooey mozzarella cheese.

Serves 4

1 teaspoon avocado oil

1 medium yellow onion, peeled and sliced

1 medium red bell pepper, seeded and sliced

¼ teaspoon ground black pepper

¼ teaspoon garlic powder

¼ teaspoon salt

4 (4-ounce) Italian sausages

4 Hot Dog Buns (see Chapter 12)

4 (1-ounce) slices mozzarella cheese

¾ cup sugar-free marinara sauce, warmed

Per Serving

Calories: 649 | Fat: 50g | Protein: 33g | Sodium: 1,678mg | Fiber: 6g | Carbohydrates: 22g | Net Carbs: 16g | Sugar: 7g

1 In a large skillet over medium heat, add oil, onion, and bell pepper. Then add black pepper, garlic powder, and salt. Stir to combine, making sure onion and bell pepper are coated completely with seasonings and oil.

2 Sauté 10–12 minutes until onion and pepper are tender, stirring occasionally. Remove from heat and set aside.

3 Lightly spray grill grate with cooking oil. Preheat grill to medium heat. Grill sausages 6–8 minutes each side until they reach an internal temperature of 160°F.

4 In each Hot Dog Bun, place 1 slice cheese, topped with 1 sausage.

5 Reheat pepper and onion on stovetop. Top each sausage with 3 tablespoons marinara sauce, then top with pepper and onion. Serve.

CHICAGO-STYLE HOT DOGS
(pictured)

Recipes for Chicago hot dogs are super specific about buns, ingredients, and the order that you put things together. In this recipe we did our best to "ketofy" it, keeping it as close as possible to the real deal.

Serves 4

4 (1.75-ounce) all-beef hot dogs

4 Hot Dog Buns (substitute poppy seeds for sesame seeds) (see Chapter 12)

4 tablespoons yellow mustard

4 tablespoons sugar-free sweet relish

4 tablespoons diced white onion

4 slices tomato, halved

4 dill pickle spears

4 pickled sport peppers

½ teaspoon celery salt

1 Lightly spray grill grate with cooking oil. Preheat grill to medium heat.

2 Grill hot dogs 4–5 minutes until fully warmed. Place in Hot Dog Buns.

3 Top evenly with mustard, relish, onion, tomato, pickles, sport peppers, and celery salt. Serve.

Per Serving

Calories: 443 | Fat: 34g | Protein: 16g | Sodium: 1,534mg | Fiber: 6g | Carbohydrates: 18g | Net Carbs: 12g | Sugar: 4g

---

BRATWURSTS IN BEER

Beer and bratwursts go hand in hand. These beer-braised bratwursts are supereasy to make and are sure to impress your friends and family! You can also use nonalcoholic beer or even broth to parboil.

Serves 4

1 (12-ounce) can beer

4 (3-ounce) uncooked bratwurst sausages

4 Hot Dog Buns (see Chapter 12)

Per Serving

Calories: 540 | Fat: 43g | Protein: 21g | Sodium: 898mg | Fiber: 4g | Carbohydrates: 12g | Net Carbs: 8g | Sugar: 2g

1 In a medium saucepan over medium heat, add beer and brats. Bring to a boil, cover, and reduce heat to a simmer. Cook covered 10 minutes. Remove brats from beer.

2 Lightly spray grill grate with cooking oil. Preheat grill to medium-high heat.

3 Grill brats 5–6 minutes until they reach an internal temperature of at least 160°F.

4 Serve in Hot Dog Buns.

BRATWURSTS WITH MUSHROOMS AND ONION

Take traditional brats to the next level by topping them with sautéed mushrooms and onion! It's a perfect way to add a few more vegetables to your diet without even noticing. If you don't like bratwurst, you can easily substitute all-beef hot dogs in this recipe.

Serves 4

½ tablespoon avocado oil

4 ounces baby bella mushrooms, sliced

1 medium yellow onion, peeled and sliced

¼ teaspoon ground black pepper

¼ teaspoon garlic powder

¼ teaspoon onion powder

¼ teaspoon salt

4 (3-ounce) uncooked bratwurst sausages

4 Hot Dog Buns (see Chapter 12)

4 tablespoons Dijon or spicy mustard

Per Serving

Calories: 602 | Fat: 46g | Protein: 23g | Sodium: 1,420mg | Fiber: 5g | Carbohydrates: 18g | Net Carbs: 13g | Sugar: 4g

1 Heat a medium skillet over medium heat. Add oil, mushrooms, and onion.

2 Add pepper, garlic powder, onion powder, and salt. Stir to combine, making sure mushrooms and onion are coated completely with seasonings and oil. Sauté 10–15 minutes until mushrooms and onion are caramelized, stirring occasionally. Remove from heat and set aside.

3 Lightly spray grill grate with cooking oil. Preheat grill to medium-high heat.

4 Grill bratwursts covered 15–20 minutes, turning occasionally, until brats reach an internal temperature of 160°F. Remove from heat.

5 Reheat mushrooms and onion. Place brats in Hot Dog Buns and top with mushrooms, onion, and mustard. Serve.

CONEY ISLAND HOT DOGS

How can you go wrong with a hot dog topped with low-carb chili? You can't. Top it with onion and mustard and dig in.

Serves 4

4 (1.75-ounce) all-beef hot dogs

4 Hot Dog Buns (see Chapter 12)

1 cup Beanless Chili (see Chapter 12), warmed

4 tablespoons yellow mustard

4 tablespoons diced white onion

Per Serving

Calories: 477 | Fat: 36g | Protein: 18g | Sodium: 958mg | Fiber: 5g | Carbohydrates: 15g | Net Carbs: 10g | Sugar: 4g

1 Lightly spray grill grate with cooking oil. Preheat grill to medium heat.

2 Grill hot dogs 4–5 minutes until fully warmed. Place in Hot Dog Buns.

3 Top each hot dog with ¼ cup Beanless Chili, 1 tablespoon mustard, and 1 tablespoon onion. Serve.

CHILI-CHEESE DOGS

Hot dogs piled high with chili and topped with shredded cheese—perfect for game days in the winter! If you'd like, you can also add some diced red onions on top.

Serves 4

4 (1.75-ounce) all-beef hot dogs

4 Hot Dog Buns (see Chapter 12)

1 cup Beanless Chili (see Chapter 12)

4 ounces Cheddar cheese, shredded

Per Serving

Calories: 579 | Fat: 44g | Protein: 24g | Sodium: 968mg | Fiber: 5g | Carbohydrates: 13g | Net Carbs: 8g | Sugar: 3g

1 Lightly spray grill grate with cooking oil. Preheat grill to medium heat.

2 Grill hot dogs 4–5 minutes until fully warmed. Place in Hot Dog Buns.

3 Top each hot dog with ¼ cup Beanless Chili and ¼ cup Cheddar. Serve.

SEATTLE HOT DOGS

(pictured)

These hot dogs are next level! Buns spread with cream cheese surround dogs topped with jalapeños, sauerkraut, and sweet Caramelized Onions.

Serves 4

4 (1.75-ounce) frankfurter hot dogs

4 medium jalapeño peppers

4 ounces full-fat cream cheese, at room temperature

4 Hot Dog Buns (see Chapter 12)

½ cup sauerkraut

¼ cup Caramelized Onions (see Chapter 5), warmed

Per Serving

Calories: 551 | Fat: 43g |
Protein: 17g | Sodium: 905mg |
Fiber: 6g | Carbohydrates: 16g |
Net Carbs: 10g | Sugar: 5g

1 Lightly spray grill grate with cooking oil. Preheat grill to medium heat.

2 Grill hot dogs and jalapeños 4–5 minutes until hot dogs are fully warmed and jalapeños are charred.

3 Spread cream cheese on Hot Dog Buns. Place hot dogs in buns.

4 Top each hot dog with 2 tablespoons sauerkraut and 1 tablespoon Caramelized Onions.

5 Slice jalapeños and top hot dogs with them. Serve.

FRENCH ONION HOT DOGS

These hot dogs are the perfect combo of savory meets sweet—smothered in Caramelized Onions and Gruyère cheese.

Serves 4

4 (1.75-ounce) all-beef hot dogs

4 Hot Dog Buns (see Chapter 12)

½ cup Caramelized Onions (see Chapter 5)

4 ounces Gruyère cheese, shredded

½ teaspoon minced fresh thyme

Per Serving

Calories: 595 | Fat: 48g |
Protein: 23g | Sodium: 1,036mg |
Fiber: 5g | Carbohydrates: 16g |
Net Carbs: 11g | Sugar: 4g

1 Lightly spray grill grate with cooking oil. Preheat grill to medium heat.

2 Grill hot dogs 4–5 minutes until fully warmed. Place in Hot Dog Buns.

3 Preheat broiler.

4 Top each hot dog with 2 tablespoons Caramelized Onions and ¼ cup Gruyère.

5 Broil hot dogs about 1–2 minutes until cheese is melted.

6 Top with fresh thyme. Serve.

CHAPTER 10

BARBECUE SEAFOOD

CEDAR PLANK SALMON

In this recipe, the woodsy aroma of cedar infuses the salmon for a very unique dish. The sweetness of Brown Sugar Dry Rub is delicious here, but feel free to play around with any seasonings you like.

Serves 4

4 (6-ounce) salmon fillets

4 teaspoons Brown Sugar Dry Rub (see Chapter 2)

Per Serving
Calories: 244 | Fat: 10g |
Protein: 34g | Sodium: 172mg |
Fiber: 0g | Carbohydrates: 3g |
Net Carbs: 1g | Sugar: 0g |
Sugar Alcohol: 2g

1 Submerge a cedar plank that's large enough to hold salmon fillets in water 1 hour. Just before grilling, remove plank from water and pat it dry.

2 Preheat grill to medium-high heat.

3 Rub Brown Sugar Dry Rub on all sides of salmon fillets.

4 Place cedar plank on grill to heat up. The plank is ready when it starts to smoke. Turn plank over and place salmon fillets on top.

5 Grill salmon covered about 10–15 minutes until it turns opaque and flakes easily with a fork.

6 Let salmon rest 5 minutes before serving.

Will the Cedar Plank Catch on Fire?

If you fully submerge the plank in water for at least an hour before grilling, it shouldn't catch on fire. But if it does, just mist it with a water bottle.

GRILLED TERIYAKI SALMON PACKETS

This easy recipe was inspired by a trip to a Japanese hibachi restaurant. To complete the experience, serve this dish along with some cauliflower rice.

Serves 4

4 (6-ounce) salmon fillets

1 medium zucchini, trimmed and sliced

2 cups broccoli florets

1 small yellow onion, peeled and sliced

4 teaspoons avocado oil

¾ teaspoon salt

¼ teaspoon ground black pepper

½ cup Hawaiian Barbecue Sauce (see Chapter 4), warmed

Per Serving

Calories: 323 | Fat: 14g | Protein: 36g | Sodium: 843mg | Fiber: 1g | Carbohydrates: 20g | Net Carbs: 7g | Sugar: 16g

1 Preheat grill to medium-high heat. Cut four (12" × 18") rectangles out of heavy-duty foil.

2 Place 1 salmon fillet in the center of each foil rectangle and evenly top with zucchini, broccoli, onion, oil, salt, and pepper.

3 Fold foil over salmon and vegetables to seal each packet.

4 Grill foil packets 5–6 minutes on each side. The fish will be opaque and flake easily with a fork when it's done.

5 Let packets rest 5 minutes before carefully opening them.

6 Serve each packet with 2 tablespoons Hawaiian Barbecue Sauce.

GRILLED LEMON-PEPPER COD PACKETS

Lemon and pepper is one of those classic flavor combinations that goes well with a lot of different things, such as roasted or grilled vegetables, chicken, and fish. For the most piquant flavor, be sure to use freshly cracked black pepper.

Serves 4

4 (6-ounce) cod fillets

½ pound asparagus, trimmed and cut into 2" pieces

½ pound yellow summer squash, trimmed and sliced

½ small yellow onion, peeled and thinly sliced

2 tablespoons extra-virgin olive oil

2 tablespoons minced fresh parsley

½ teaspoon salt

½ teaspoon freshly cracked black pepper

4 lemon slices

4 lemon wedges

Per Serving

Calories: 204 | Fat: 7g | Protein: 28g | Sodium: 809mg | Fiber: 2g | Carbohydrates: 6g | Net Carbs: 4g | Sugar: 3g

1 Preheat grill to medium-high heat. Cut four (12" × 18") rectangles out of heavy-duty foil.

2 Place 1 cod fillet in the center of each foil rectangle and evenly top with vegetables, oil, parsley, salt, and pepper. Put 1 lemon slice on top of each.

3 Fold foil over cod and vegetables to seal each packet.

4 Grill foil packets 5–6 minutes on each side. The fish will be opaque and flake easily with a fork when it's done.

5 Let packets rest 5 minutes before carefully opening them. Serve each portion with a lemon wedge to squeeze on top.

GRILLED GARLIC BUTTER SHRIMP

Grilled garlicky shrimp dripping with butter is one of life's simple pleasures. Serve this with a leafy green salad to make it a meal, or with your favorite keto-friendly "noodles."

Serves 4

1¼ pounds peeled and deveined medium shrimp
1½ tablespoons avocado oil
1½ tablespoons fresh lemon juice
½ teaspoon salt
½ teaspoon ground black pepper
1 medium lemon, halved
3 tablespoons salted butter
1 medium clove garlic, peeled and crushed
1 tablespoon minced fresh parsley

Per Serving
Calories: 226 | Fat: 14g |
Protein: 20g | Sodium: 1,161mg |
Fiber: 0g | Carbohydrates: 2g |
Net Carbs: 2g | Sugar: 0g

1 In a large bowl, add shrimp, oil, lemon juice, salt, and pepper. Toss to coat. Cover bowl and let shrimp marinate in the refrigerator 15 minutes.

2 Soak ten wooden skewers in water 20 minutes. Lightly spray grill grate with cooking oil. Preheat grill to medium-high heat.

3 Thread shrimp onto soaked wooden skewers.

4 Grill shrimp skewers about 2 minutes per side until opaque, flipping once. After flipping shrimp, place lemon halves (cut side down) onto grill and cook 1–2 minutes until charred.

5 In a small skillet over medium heat, add butter. Once melted, add garlic and cook, stirring constantly, 30–60 seconds until fragrant. Turn off heat and stir in parsley.

6 Serve shrimp warm along with garlic butter for dipping and charred lemon halves to squeeze on top.

Can You Reheat Shrimp?

Yes! To do so, add shrimp and a splash of water to a preheated skillet over high heat and cook until warm, stirring frequently. This shouldn't take more than a couple of minutes.

GRILLED LIME SHRIMP PACKETS

Fresh lime juice and zest pack a nice punch of flavor with grilled shrimp. Feel free to add different-colored bell pepper or other vegetables, such as broccoli or cauliflower, if you want.

Serves 4

1¼ pounds peeled and deveined medium shrimp

1 medium red bell pepper, seeded and thinly sliced

1 medium clove garlic, peeled and crushed

2 tablespoons avocado oil

2 tablespoons fresh lime juice

2 teaspoons fresh lime zest

½ teaspoon salt

½ teaspoon ground black pepper

4 tablespoons fresh cilantro leaves

1 medium avocado, peeled, pitted, and thinly sliced

1 medium lime, quartered

Per Serving
Calories: 215 | Fat: 11g | Protein: 20g | Sodium: 1,096mg | Fiber: 3g | Carbohydrates: 7g | Net Carbs: 4g | Sugar: 2g

1 In a large bowl, add shrimp, bell pepper, garlic, oil, lime juice, lime zest, salt, and black pepper. Toss to coat. Cover bowl and let shrimp marinate in the refrigerator 15 minutes.

2 Preheat grill to medium-high heat. Cut four (12" × 18") rectangles out of heavy-duty foil.

3 Divide shrimp mixture (with juices) evenly among foil rectangles. Fold foil over shrimp to seal each packet.

4 Grill foil packets 5–6 minutes on each side. The shrimp will be opaque when it's done.

5 Let packets rest 5 minutes before carefully opening them. Serve each portion topped with 1 tablespoon cilantro leaves and ¼ avocado slices along with 1 lime wedge to squeeze on top.

Make It a Meal

Grilled Lime Shrimp Packets are perfect for serving with cauliflower rice! And if you want, a sprinkle of crumbled feta or queso fresco on top is delicious.

GRILLED WHOLE SNAPPER

Impress your guests with this easy keto recipe! If you've never grilled a whole fish before, you'll be surprised at how effortless it really is. The key is to make sure it's done in the center; use a meat thermometer to ensure the fish reaches an internal temperature of 145°F.

Serves 4

1 (3-pound) whole red snapper, scaled and cleaned
3 tablespoons extra-virgin olive oil
3 tablespoons fresh lemon juice
¾ teaspoon salt
½ teaspoon ground black pepper
4 lemon wedges

Per Serving
Calories: 242 | Fat: 11g |
Protein: 31g | Sodium: 531mg |
Fiber: 0g | Carbohydrates: 1g |
Net Carbs: 1g | Sugar: 0g

1 Make four (3") slashes on both sides of fish.

2 In a small bowl, whisk together oil, lemon juice, salt, and pepper. Rub mixture into both sides of fish.

3 Lightly spray grill grate with cooking oil. Preheat grill to medium-high heat.

4 Grill fish, flipping once, about 20 minutes until flesh is opaque, flakes easily with a fork, and has reached an internal temperature of 145°F.

5 Serve fish warm with lemon wedges to squeeze on top. Be careful of the bones!

Switch Up the Flavor Profile

Instead of the salt and pepper in this recipe, use 3 tablespoons of our Southwest Dry Rub (see Chapter 2). Alternatively, you could use one batch of Asian Marinade or Garlic and Herb Marinade (both in Chapter 3) instead of the extra-virgin olive oil, lemon juice, salt, and black pepper in this recipe.

GRILLED TUNA SALAD

(pictured)

The Asian flavor profile in this recipe pairs perfectly with tuna steaks. You can make the Vinaigrette Coleslaw up to 5 days ahead, but note that it will lose some of its crispness. Don't cook the tuna ahead of time, though. Because it is left rare in the center, we recommend grilling the tuna just before serving.

Serves 4

1 batch Vinaigrette Coleslaw (see Chapter 11)
1 batch Grilled Ahi Tuna (see recipe in this chapter)
1 medium avocado, peeled, pitted, and thinly sliced
4 tablespoons chopped fresh cilantro
2 teaspoons sesame seeds

1. Divide Vinaigrette Coleslaw evenly among four plates.

2. Top each with 1 sliced Grilled Ahi Tuna steak.

3. Top steaks evenly with avocado, cilantro, and sesame seeds. Serve.

Per Serving
Calories: 424 | Fat: 19g | Protein: 47g | Sodium: 1,582mg | Fiber: 6g | Carbohydrates: 16g | Net Carbs: 7g | Sugar: 3g | Sugar Alcohol: 3g

---

GRILLED SCALLOPS

Seasonings are kept to a minimum here to allow the flavor of the scallops to really shine through. Be sure to look for the freshest scallops you can find.

Serves 4

1¼ pounds large uncooked sea scallops
1½ tablespoons extra-virgin olive oil
¼ teaspoon salt
¼ teaspoon ground black pepper
4 lemon wedges

1. In a large bowl, add all ingredients except lemon wedges and toss to coat.

2. Lightly spray grill grate with cooking oil. Preheat grill to medium-high heat.

3. Grill scallops about 2–3 minutes per side until opaque and grill marks are visible.

4. Serve warm with lemon wedges to squeeze on top.

Per Serving
Calories: 142 | Fat: 5g | Protein: 17g | Sodium: 700mg | Fiber: 0g | Carbohydrates: 5g | Net Carbs: 5g | Sugar: 0g

GRILLED SHRIMP PO'BOYS

(pictured)

This keto version of a traditional po'boy uses our Hot Dog Buns in place of baguettes and Creamy Coleslaw in place of lettuce and rémoulade for a slightly different, but equally delicious, flavor profile.

Serves 4

½ batch Creamy Coleslaw (see Chapter 11)

4 Hot Dog Buns, sliced open lengthwise (see Chapter 12)

1 batch Smoky Paprika Shrimp (see recipe in this chapter), warmed

1 Divide Creamy Coleslaw equally among Hot Dog Buns.

2 Top each with Smoky Paprika Dry Rub Grilled Shrimp. Serve.

Per Serving

Calories: 524 | Fat: 37g | Protein: 30g | Sodium: 1,435mg | Fiber: 6g | Carbohydrates: 17g | Net Carbs: 10g | Sugar: 4g | Sugar Alcohol: 1g

---

SMOKY PAPRIKA SHRIMP

Smoked paprika from the dry rub adds great depth of flavor here. Serve this shrimp on a bed of greens to make it a meal, or serve as an appetizer along with Green Goddess Dressing or Ranch (see recipes in Chapter 5) for dipping.

Serves 4

1¼ pounds peeled and deveined medium shrimp

1½ tablespoons avocado oil

1 tablespoon apple cider vinegar

5 teaspoons Smoky Paprika Dry Rub (see Chapter 2)

Per Serving

Calories: 154 | Fat: 6g | Protein: 20g | Sodium: 986mg | Fiber: 1g | Carbohydrates: 3g | Net Carbs: 1g | Sugar: 0g | Sugar Alcohol: 1g

1 In a large bowl, add all ingredients and toss to coat. Cover bowl and let shrimp marinate in the refrigerator 15 minutes.

2 Soak ten wooden skewers in water 20 minutes. Preheat grill to medium-high heat.

3 Thread shrimp onto soaked wooden skewers.

4 Grill shrimp skewers about 2 minutes per side until opaque. Serve warm.

GRILLED AHI TUNA

This restaurant-quality dish only looks difficult to make, when in reality it couldn't be easier. The only trick to this recipe is to make sure you don't overcook the steaks; they should be rare in the center.

Serves 4

4 (6-ounce, 1"-thick) sushi-grade ahi tuna steaks

1½ batches Asian Marinade (see Chapter 3)

4 tablespoons fresh cilantro leaves

4 lime wedges

Per Serving

Calories: 203 | Fat: 1g | Protein: 44g | Sodium: 1,208mg | Fiber: 0g | Carbohydrates: 7g | Net Carbs: 4g | Sugar: 0g | Sugar Alcohol: 3g

1 In a large bowl, add tuna steaks and Asian Marinade and toss to coat. Cover bowl and let tuna marinate 5 minutes.

2 Lightly spray grill grate with cooking oil. Preheat grill to medium-high heat.

3 Grill tuna steaks about 2–3 minutes per side until seared.

4 Let fish rest 3 minutes before thinly slicing.

5 Sprinkle with cilantro leaves and serve warm along with lime wedges to squeeze on top.

Does This Recipe Require Sushi-Grade Tuna?

You should use sushi-grade tuna for this dish. The outside of the tuna steaks is seared, but the inside is served rare, so you should use an excellent-quality fish. Be careful not to overcook the tuna, or it will be tough and dry.

CHAPTER 11

SALADS

CREAMY COLESLAW

When thinking of barbecue side dishes, it doesn't get any more classic than coleslaw! While traditional versions are filled with sugar, this keto version will satisfy your cravings without knocking you out of ketosis. Pair this with any of the meat dishes in this book, like Pulled Barbecue Chicken Breasts (see Chapter 6), Shredded Pork Butt (see Chapter 7), or Grilled Beef Ribs (see Chapter 8). Anything you can grill up and serve with barbecue sauce is great with this coleslaw!

Serves 8

½ cup full-fat mayonnaise
2 tablespoons apple cider vinegar
½ tablespoon Dijon mustard
½ tablespoon poppy seeds
½ teaspoon salt
¼ teaspoon ground black pepper
7 drops liquid stevia
4 cups thinly sliced savoy cabbage
1 cup thinly sliced red cabbage
½ small white onion, peeled and thinly sliced
½ cup chopped fresh parsley

Per Serving
Calories: 114 | Fat: 10g |
Protein: 1g | Sodium: 270mg |
Fiber: 2g | Carbohydrates: 4g |
Net Carbs: 2g | Sugar: 2g

1 In a large bowl, whisk together mayonnaise, vinegar, mustard, poppy seeds, salt, pepper, and stevia.

2 Stir in remaining ingredients and mix well to combine. Serve immediately or, if you prefer, refrigerate 20 minutes before serving.

Make This Dish Ahead

This dish can be made up to three days in advance and stored covered in the refrigerator. Note that the cabbage will soften the longer it sits.

VINAIGRETTE COLESLAW

This lighter take on coleslaw is a refreshing change of pace from our more traditional Creamy Coleslaw (see recipe in this chapter). You can serve it with just about anything you grill, but it's particularly delicious with fish.

Serves 8

¼ cup avocado oil

3 tablespoons apple cider vinegar

½ tablespoon Dijon mustard

½ teaspoon salt

¼ teaspoon ground black pepper

7 drops liquid stevia

5 cups thinly sliced or shredded savoy cabbage

1 small carrot, peeled and shredded

1 medium scallion, trimmed and thinly sliced

1 In a large bowl, whisk together oil, vinegar, mustard, salt, pepper, and stevia.

2 Stir in remaining ingredients and mix well to combine.

3 Serve immediately or, if you prefer, refrigerate 20 minutes before serving. Store covered in the refrigerator up to 3 days.

Per Serving

Calories: 81 | Fat: 7g | Protein: 1g | Sodium: 190mg | Fiber: 2g | Carbohydrates: 4g | Net Carbs: 2g | Sugar: 2g

---

BLUE CHEESE– PECAN SLAW

Savory blue cheese and toasted pecans make this slaw something truly special! If you want to take it to the next level, crumble more blue cheese on top right before serving. It's the perfect keto meal paired with a steak hot off the grill!

Serves 6

6 cups thinly sliced Brussels sprouts (about 1 pound)

¾ cup Blue Cheese Dressing (see Chapter 5)

1 medium scallion, trimmed and thinly sliced

¼ cup pecans, toasted

In a large bowl, toss together all ingredients. Serve.

Per Serving

Calories: 185 | Fat: 15g | Protein: 5g | Sodium: 195mg | Fiber: 4g | Carbohydrates: 9g | Net Carbs: 5g | Sugar: 3g

CAULIFLOWER "POTATO" SALAD

You won't believe how close our mock potato salad is to the real deal! You won't even miss the potato. Don't skip the dill pickles; they really make this side dish something special.

Serves 6

3 cups cauliflower florets

6 tablespoons full-fat mayonnaise

2 tablespoons finely minced dill pickles

1 teaspoon yellow mustard

1 teaspoon onion powder

1 teaspoon garlic powder

½ teaspoon salt

¼ teaspoon ground sweet paprika

⅛ teaspoon ground black pepper

¼ cup minced red onion

2 large eggs, hard-boiled and chopped

2 tablespoons chopped fresh dill

Per Serving

Calories: 139 | Fat: 12g | Protein: 4g | Sodium: 351mg | Fiber: 1g | Carbohydrates: 4g | Net Carbs: 3g | Sugar: 2g

1 In a medium saucepan over medium-high heat, add cauliflower and enough water to cover by 2"–3". Bring to a boil, then reduce heat and simmer about 5 minutes until fork-tender. Drain and cool completely.

2 In a large bowl, whisk together mayonnaise, pickles, mustard, onion powder, garlic powder, salt, paprika, pepper, and onion. Add cauliflower, eggs, and dill, and stir to combine.

3 Cover and refrigerate 1 hour or up to 5 days before serving.

Why Does This Need to Be Chilled for an Hour?

The flavor of this salad is even better after the flavors have had the chance to blend a bit. This dish is perfect for meal prep or to make ahead and bring to an outdoor barbecue!

JALAPEÑO-RANCH SLAW

Jalapeños add kick and Ranch dressing cools it down; this slaw has the best of both worlds! Part of what makes this dish so delicious is using homemade Ranch. However, if you don't have time, you can use low-carb store-bought ranch dressing instead.

Serves 8

¾ cup **Ranch (see Chapter 5)**
5 cups thinly sliced green cabbage
1 cup thinly sliced red cabbage
½ small white onion, peeled and thinly sliced
1 medium jalapeño pepper, seeded and minced
½ cup chopped fresh parsley

In a large bowl, stir together all ingredients. Serve.

Per Serving

Calories: 126 | Fat: 12g | Protein: 1g | Sodium: 136mg | Fiber: 2g | Carbohydrates: 5g | Net Carbs: 3g | Sugar: 2g

---

GREEK SALAD

Just like what you'd find at a Greek diner, this salad is bursting with flavors and textures! To add a smoky dimension, grill the romaine lettuce first.

Serves 4

2 tablespoons extra-virgin olive oil
2 tablespoons fresh lemon juice
1 tablespoon chopped fresh oregano
¼ teaspoon salt
⅛ teaspoon ground black pepper
6 cups chopped romaine lettuce
¼ medium English cucumber, chopped
1 cup cherry tomatoes, halved
½ small red onion, peeled and thinly sliced
¼ cup kalamata olives, pitted and halved
2 ounces feta cheese, crumbled or cubed

1 In a large bowl, whisk together oil, lemon juice, oregano, salt, and pepper.

2 Add lettuce, cucumber, tomatoes, onion, and olives. Toss gently to combine.

3 Sprinkle with feta and serve.

Per Serving

Calories: 152 | Fat: 13g | Protein: 3g | Sodium: 474mg | Fiber: 2g | Carbohydrates: 7g | Net Carbs: 5g | Sugar: 3g

GRILLED CAESAR SALAD

If you've never grilled romaine lettuce before, you're in for a real treat. Not only does it take on a smoky flavor, but it gets beautiful char marks. If you like a chicken or steak Caesar salad, go for it and grill up your favorite meat as well!

Serves 4

2 medium heads romaine lettuce, cut in half lengthwise

Avocado oil spray

½ cup Caesar Dressing (see Chapter 5)

1 ounce Parmesan cheese, shaved

Per Serving
Calories: 198 | Fat: 14g | Protein: 8g | Sodium: 313mg | Fiber: 7g | Carbohydrates: 11g | Net Carbs: 4g | Sugar: 4g

1 Preheat grill to medium-high heat.

2 Spray both sides of each romaine head half with avocado oil.

3 Place lettuce (cut side down) on grill and cook 2–3 minutes on the first side and 1–2 minutes on the second side until grill marks are visible.

4 Drizzle Caesar Dressing on top and sprinkle with Parmesan. Serve.

Can You Grill the Lettuce in Advance?

Once you grill lettuce, it will keep fine in the refrigerator for a day. However, we prefer to eat it right after grilling for the best texture.

TOMATO-CUCUMBER SALAD

(pictured)

Growing up, we frequently ate Italian chopped salad. It was just chopped cucumber and tomato tossed with store-bought Italian dressing! That childhood recipe served as the inspiration for this lower-carb version. To make this a full meal, try serving it with grilled chicken and a sprinkle of crumbled feta.

Serves 6

2 tablespoons extra-virgin olive oil
1 tablespoon red wine vinegar
¼ teaspoon salt
¼ teaspoon ground black pepper
½ medium English cucumber, chopped
2 medium tomatoes, cored and chopped
½ small red onion, peeled and thinly sliced
2 tablespoons minced fresh parsley

1 In a large bowl, whisk together oil, vinegar, salt, and pepper.

2 Add cucumber, tomatoes, onion, and parsley and toss together all ingredients. Serve.

Per Serving

Calories: 53 | Fat: 4g | Protein: 1g | Sodium: 100mg | Fiber: 1g | Carbohydrates: 3g | Net Carbs: 2g | Sugar: 2g

---

CREAMY CUCUMBER SALAD

If you think cucumber isn't your thing, you need to try it in this salad. With a slightly tangy sour cream base and the addition of white onion and fresh dill, it's perfect in its simplicity. If you have a little feta or goat cheese in the refrigerator, try crumbling some on top.

Serves 6

⅓ cup full-fat sour cream
1 tablespoon white wine vinegar
½ teaspoon salt
⅛ teaspoon ground white pepper
1 medium English cucumber, thinly sliced
½ small white onion, peeled and thinly sliced
3 tablespoons chopped fresh dill

1 In a large bowl, whisk together sour cream, vinegar, salt, and pepper.

2 Stir in remaining ingredients. Serve.

Per Serving

Calories: 34 | Fat: 2g | Protein: 1g | Sodium: 201mg | Fiber: 0g | Carbohydrates: 3g | Net Carbs: 3g | Sugar: 2g

GRILLED WATERMELON-FETA SALAD

(pictured)

This salad is something you should make at least once every summer! The only trick is to use a watermelon that's freshly cut. If you cut it and leave it for a few days in the refrigerator, it starts to get soft and will be harder to grill.

Serves 4

3 cups cubed watermelon
Avocado oil spray
2 ounces feta cheese, crumbled
4 teaspoons chopped fresh mint
2 lime wedges

Per Serving
Calories: 81 | Fat: 4g |
Protein: 3g | Sodium: 130mg |
Fiber: 1g | Carbohydrates: 9g |
Net Carbs: 8g | Sugar: 8g

1 Submerge four wooden skewers in water 20 minutes. Preheat grill to medium-high.

2 Skewer watermelon onto skewers. Lightly spray with avocado oil.

3 Grill skewers 2–3 minutes on the first side and 1–2 minutes on the second side until grill marks appear.

4 Place in a large bowl, sprinkle with feta and mint, and squeeze lime wedges over top. Serve.

BLUE CHEESE– CELERY SLAW

Celery ribs cut into crispy, crunchy little half-moons and then tossed with homemade luscious Blue Cheese Dressing is a surprisingly addictive way to enjoy celery. To take this salad over the top, sprinkle on 1 ounce crumbled blue cheese right before serving.

Serves 6

5 large stalks celery, trimmed and thinly sliced
¾ cup Blue Cheese Dressing (see Chapter 5)
1 small carrot, peeled and shredded
2 medium scallions, trimmed and thinly sliced

In a large bowl, toss together all ingredients. Serve.

Per Serving
Calories: 129 | Fat: 12g | Protein: 2g | Sodium: 222mg | Fiber: 1g | Carbohydrates: 3g | Net Carbs: 2g | Sugar: 2g

CHAPTER 12

SIDE DISHES

LOADED MASHED "POTATOES"

Cauliflower mashed potatoes aren't anything new in the keto world, but this version has a couple of tweaks that really make it something special. For starters, the garlic is cooked and mashed right in with the cauliflower to add savory flavor. Also, a food processor is used to puree everything so it's silky smooth and velvety. And of course the "potatoes" are loaded up with Cheddar, sour cream, bacon, and chives!

Serves 5

1 pound cauliflower florets
2 medium cloves garlic, peeled
2 tablespoons unsalted butter
¼ teaspoon salt
⅛ teaspoon ground black pepper
¼ cup shredded Cheddar cheese
2 tablespoons full-fat sour cream
2 slices no-sugar-added bacon, cooked crispy and crumbled
4 teaspoons minced fresh chives

Per Serving
Calories: 118 | Fat: 9g |
Protein: 5g | Sodium: 260mg |
Fiber: 2g | Carbohydrates: 5g |
Net Carbs: 3g | Sugar: 2g

1 In a medium saucepan over medium-high heat, add cauliflower and garlic and cover with cold water. Bring to a boil, then reduce heat to medium. Continue cooking covered about 8 minutes until cauliflower is easily mashable. Drain well.

2 In a food processor, add cauliflower and garlic, butter, salt, and pepper. Process until smooth. Stir in Cheddar.

3 Transfer to a serving dish and top with sour cream, crumbled bacon, and chives. Serve warm.

BACON-SAUTÉED GREEN BEANS

Smoky bacon, tangy balsamic, and a hint of sweetness make this green bean dish not your average keto side. Don't tell anyone, but we've been known to make a double batch and call it dinner.

Serves 4

4 slices no-sugar-added bacon

1 pound fresh green beans, trimmed

½ cup chicken stock

1 tablespoon good-quality balsamic vinegar

½ teaspoon granulated monk fruit–erythritol blend

⅛ teaspoon salt

⅛ teaspoon ground black pepper

Per Serving
Calories: 99 | Fat: 4g |
Protein: 7g | Sodium: 315mg |
Fiber: 3g | Carbohydrates: 9g |
Net Carbs: 6g | Sugar: 4g

1 In a medium skillet over medium heat, cook bacon until crisp. Transfer to a plate to cool, and then crumble. Leave fat in skillet.

2 Return skillet to stove, increasing heat to medium-high. Add green beans, stock, vinegar, monk fruit–erythritol, salt, and pepper. Bring to a boil and then cover skillet, reduce heat to medium, and cook 5 minutes.

3 Uncover and cook 2–3 minutes until liquid is evaporated, stirring occasionally.

4 Transfer to a serving dish and sprinkle with crumbled bacon. Serve warm.

LEMONY COLLARD GREENS

The key to cooking greens is to make sure they're not bitter. The first trick is to start with smaller leaves, which are younger, and then add other ingredients to complement the greens' delicious flavor. Here chicken stock adds depth, garlic and crushed red pepper flakes add savory spice, and lemon wakes everything up.

Serves 4

4 slices no-sugar-added bacon

2 pounds fresh collard greens, trimmed and chopped

2 medium cloves garlic, peeled and minced

½ cup chicken stock

¼ teaspoon crushed red pepper flakes

⅛ teaspoon salt

⅛ teaspoon ground black pepper

4 lemon wedges

Per Serving

Calories: 120 | Fat: 5g |
Protein: 10g | Sodium: 337mg |
Fiber: 7g | Carbohydrates: 11g |
Net Carbs: 4g | Sugar: 1g

1 In a large skillet over medium heat, cook bacon until crisp. Transfer to a plate to cool, and then crumble. Leave fat in skillet.

2 Return skillet to medium heat and add collard greens, garlic, stock, red pepper flakes, salt, and black pepper. Cover skillet and cook 10–12 minutes until greens are tender.

3 Uncover and cook 2–3 minutes until liquid is evaporated, stirring occasionally.

4 Transfer to a serving dish and sprinkle with crumbled bacon. Serve warm with lemon wedges for squeezing on top.

What to Look for When Buying Collard Greens

Look for green, firm collard greens, avoiding heads with brown and wilted leaves. The smaller the leaves, the younger, more tender, and less bitter the greens. And bonus: Younger greens cook up faster too!

GRILLED GARLICKY SUMMER SQUASH

If you have a garden with summer squash, this simple recipe is one of the best things you can make with it! Feel free to swap out the yellow summer squash for zucchini if that's what you have on hand, but note that the nutrition information may change.

Serves 6

3 tablespoons extra-virgin olive oil

2 medium cloves garlic, peeled and minced

⅓ teaspoon salt

¼ teaspoon ground black pepper

2 pounds yellow summer squash, trimmed and sliced into ¼" slices

2 tablespoons fresh sliced basil (thinly sliced chiffonade style)

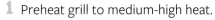

Per Serving
Calories: 84 | Fat: 7g |
Protein: 2g | Sodium: 132mg |
Fiber: 2g | Carbohydrates: 5g |
Net Carbs: 3g | Sugar: 3g

1 Preheat grill to medium-high heat.

2 In a large bowl, whisk together oil, garlic, salt, and pepper. Add sliced squash and toss to coat.

3 Grill squash about 5 minutes per side until tender and grill marks are visible.

4 Transfer to a serving platter and sprinkle with basil. Serve hot or cold.

What Is Summer Squash?

Summer squash refers to the variety of squashes that are harvested during the summer. They typically have a tender, edible rind as compared with the harder, inedible rind of some winter squash.

GRILLED BELL PEPPERS

You're going to love how easy it is to grill a batch of bell peppers! Once they're grilled, let them cool a bit and then thinly slice them and use them to make fajitas, add them to a salad, or smother a burger with them.

Serves 4

2 medium green bell peppers, seeded and cut in half lengthwise
Olive oil spray
⅛ teaspoon salt
⅛ teaspoon ground black pepper

Per Serving
Calories: 21 | Fat: 1g |
Protein: 1g | Sodium: 74mg |
Fiber: 1g | Carbohydrates: 3g |
Net Carbs: 2g | Sugar: 1g

1 Preheat grill to medium-high heat.

2 Lightly spray each bell pepper half with oil and sprinkle with salt and black pepper.

3 Grill peppers 3–5 minutes per side until tender and grill marks are visible.

4 Serve hot or cold.

Try Red, Yellow, or Orange Bell Peppers

Grill other varieties of bell peppers the same way you grill green peppers. However, note that nutrition information may differ for different varieties.

GRILLED MARINATED EGGPLANT

The beauty of eggplant is that it absorbs the flavors of whatever it's cooked with. You can experiment with this marinade using different types of vinegar, spices, and herb garnishes to come up with different flavor profiles.

Serves 4

3 tablespoons extra-virgin olive oil

1½ tablespoons red wine vinegar

1 medium clove garlic, peeled and minced

¼ teaspoon crushed red pepper flakes

¼ teaspoon salt

¼ teaspoon ground black pepper

1 pound eggplant, trimmed and sliced into ¼" circles

1 tablespoon minced fresh parsley

Per Serving
Calories: 115 | Fat: 10g |
Protein: 1g | Sodium: 147mg |
Fiber: 3g | Carbohydrates: 6g |
Net Carbs: 3g | Sugar: 3g

1 In a small bowl, whisk together oil, vinegar, garlic, red pepper flakes, salt, and black pepper.

2 Pour oil mixture into a large zip-top bag and add eggplant. Seal the bag and move eggplant around until coated. Let eggplant marinate 15 minutes. Drain and discard marinade.

3 Preheat grill to medium-high heat.

4 Grill eggplant 2–5 minutes per side until tender and grill marks are visible.

5 Transfer to a serving platter and sprinkle with parsley. Serve hot or cold.

Serving This Dish

You can serve this as a side dish with any meat you grill! Another idea is to serve it as part of a low-carb cheese board, charcuterie board, or Italian antipasto platter.

CHEDDAR CAULIFLOWER "MAC" AND CHEESE

This is one side dish that needs no introduction. Mac and cheese is probably most people's favorite side, and this keto version rivals the traditional! With a rich and creamy cheese sauce, you won't miss the mac. Feel free to swap out the sharp Cheddar for what you like; Gouda and Gruyère are also wonderful here.

Serves 10

2 pounds cauliflower florets

2 tablespoons unsalted butter, at room temperature

¼ cup heavy whipping cream

2 tablespoons water

1 teaspoon Worcestershire sauce

1 teaspoon onion powder

½ teaspoon garlic powder

½ teaspoon Dijon mustard

½ teaspoon hot sauce

¼ teaspoon salt

¼ teaspoon ground black pepper

4 ounces full-fat cream cheese, at room temperature

6 ounces sharp Cheddar cheese, shredded

Per Serving

Calories: 172 | Fat: 13g | Protein: 7g | Sodium: 258mg | Fiber: 2g | Carbohydrates: 6g | Net Carbs: 4g | Sugar: 2g

1 In a medium saucepan over medium-high heat, add cauliflower and cover with cold water. Bring to a boil, then reduce heat to medium. Cook covered about 5 minutes until cauliflower is fork-tender. Drain well.

2 In a separate medium saucepan over medium heat, add butter, cream, water, Worcestershire, onion powder, garlic powder, mustard, hot sauce, salt, pepper, and cream cheese. Cook about 5 minutes until smooth and creamy, whisking occasionally. Whisk in Cheddar a handful at a time until fully incorporated.

3 In a large serving dish, stir together drained cauliflower and cheese sauce. Serve warm.

BEANLESS CHILI

Chili-cheese dog, anyone? Use this Beanless Chili to top hot dogs or to make a taco salad, or eat it as is with a spoon! If you're going the spoon route, a generous sprinkle of shredded Cheddar or a dollop of sour cream goes well on top.

Serves 8

1 tablespoon avocado oil

½ pound 85/15 lean ground beef

½ pound mild ground Italian sausage

1 medium stalk celery, trimmed and chopped

1 medium green bell pepper, seeded and chopped

½ medium yellow onion, peeled and chopped

5 medium cloves garlic, peeled and crushed

2 cups beef stock

5 tablespoons tomato paste

½ tablespoon chili powder

1 teaspoon dried oregano

1 teaspoon ground cumin

¼ teaspoon ground turmeric

¼ teaspoon ground black pepper

Per Serving

Calories: 200 | Fat: 14g | Protein: 11g | Sodium: 445mg | Fiber: 1g | Carbohydrates: 5g | Net Carbs: 4g | Sugar: 2g

1 In a large pot over high heat, add oil, ground beef, and sausage. Cook about 5 minutes until meat is browned, stirring occasionally to break up meat.

2 Reduce heat to medium-high. Stir in celery, bell pepper, onion, and garlic, and cook about 5 minutes until vegetables are slightly softened, stirring frequently.

3 Stir in stock, tomato paste, chili powder, oregano, cumin, turmeric, and black pepper. Bring to a boil. Cover pot, reduce heat to simmer, and cook 15 minutes, stirring frequently.

4 Serve immediately or store refrigerated up to 4 days.

JALAPEÑO-CHEDDAR "CORN BREAD"

This keto "corn bread" pairs perfectly with many barbecue meats and will satisfy your corn bread cravings! The salty, tangy Cheddar is a perfect pairing with piquant jalapeño peppers. This has about a "medium" spice level, but feel free to add more or fewer jalapeños to suit your taste.

Serves 12

1 cup almond flour
2 tablespoons coconut flour
1½ teaspoons baking powder
¼ teaspoon salt
¼ teaspoon garlic powder
⅛ teaspoon ground black pepper
2 large eggs
½ cup whole milk
½ teaspoon apple cider vinegar
3 drops liquid stevia
6 tablespoons unsalted butter, melted and cooled slightly
2 medium jalapeño peppers, seeded and minced
1 medium scallion, trimmed and thinly sliced
4 ounces Cheddar cheese, shredded

Per Serving
Calories: 173 | Fat: 14g |
Protein: 6g | Sodium: 188mg |
Fiber: 2g | Carbohydrates: 3g |
Net Carbs: 1g | Sugar: 1g

1. Preheat oven to 350°F.

2. Line an 8½" × 4¼" loaf pan with parchment paper. Lightly spray parchment with avocado oil.

3. In a large bowl, whisk together almond flour, coconut flour, baking powder, salt, garlic powder, and black pepper.

4. In a medium bowl, whisk together eggs, milk, vinegar, stevia, and butter.

5. Beat wet ingredients into dry ingredients. Fold in jalapeños, scallion, and Cheddar.

6. Transfer batter to prepared loaf pan. Use a spatula to smooth the top.

7. Bake 50 minutes until a wooden pick inserted in the center comes out dry or with just a few crumbs.

8. Cool completely before slicing and serving.

How Long Will Corn Bread Keep?

If you wrap this bread well and store it in the refrigerator, it should keep up to 1 week. After it's been refrigerated, we like to toast the slices under the broiler before serving.

HOT DOG BUNS

These buns are what your hot dogs and sausages have been missing! These soft, breadlike buns are a pretty golden color thanks to the addition of a touch of turmeric. Basting them with melted butter straight out of the oven is what makes them completely irresistible.

Serves 4

½ teaspoon instant yeast

2 teaspoons warm water

1 teaspoon beef gelatin powder

1½ tablespoons plus ¼ cup boiling water, divided

¾ cup almond flour

3 tablespoons coconut flour

4 teaspoons psyllium husk powder

1 teaspoon baking powder

½ teaspoon salt

¼ teaspoon ground turmeric

2 large egg whites

2 tablespoons unsalted butter, melted

1 tablespoon apple cider vinegar

5 drops liquid stevia

1 tablespoon salted butter, melted

Per Serving

Calories: 256 | Fat: 20g | Protein: 9g | Sodium: 179mg | Fiber: 4g | Carbohydrates: 10g | Net Carbs: 6g | Sugar: 2g

1 Preheat oven to 350°F.

2 In a small bowl, add yeast and warm water and stir to combine. Let it sit 5–10 minutes until foamy.

3 In a separate small bowl, add gelatin powder and 1½ tablespoons boiling water and stir to dissolve gelatin powder.

4 In a large bowl, whisk together almond flour, coconut flour, psyllium husk powder, baking powder, salt, and turmeric.

5 In a medium bowl, whisk together egg whites, unsalted melted butter, vinegar, stevia, yeast mixture, and dissolved gelatin powder.

6 Stir egg mixture into dry ingredients and then stir in remaining ¼ cup boiling water.

7 Let batter rest 3 minutes to thicken. Divide batter into four equal parts and roll each into a ball. (You can oil your hands if the dough is sticky.) Use your hands to roll each dough ball into a log about 5½" long. Place dough logs evenly spaced out on an ungreased baking sheet.

8 Bake about 30 minutes until buns are golden brown on top and bottom.

9 Remove buns from oven and brush melted butter on top.

10 Turn off oven, return buns to oven, and let buns cool completely with oven door slightly ajar.

11 Serve immediately or store in a zip-top plastic bag in the refrigerator up to 1 week.

HAMBURGER BUNS

These buns have a delicious breadlike flavor with a soft interior. Don't skip the sesame seeds on top—they give them a real bun feel! Because of how nutritionally dense keto food is, these Hamburger Buns are small. Each bun is about 2½" in diameter, so they're slider size.

Serves 4

½ teaspoon instant yeast

2 teaspoons warm water

1 teaspoon beef gelatin powder

1½ tablespoons plus ¼ cup boiling water, divided

¾ cup almond flour

3 tablespoons coconut flour

4 teaspoons psyllium husk powder

1 teaspoon baking powder

½ teaspoon salt

3 large egg whites, divided

2 tablespoons unsalted butter, melted

1 tablespoon apple cider vinegar

5 drops liquid stevia

¾ teaspoon sesame seeds

Per Serving
Calories: 237 | Fat: 17g |
Protein: 10g | Sodium: 461mg |
Fiber: 4g | Carbohydrates: 10g |
Net Carbs: 6g | Sugar: 2g

1 Preheat oven to 350°F.

2 In a small bowl, add yeast and warm water and stir to combine. Let it sit 5–10 minutes until foamy.

3 In a separate small bowl, add gelatin powder and 1½ tablespoons boiling water and stir to dissolve.

4 In a large bowl, whisk together almond flour, coconut flour, psyllium husk powder, baking powder, and salt.

5 In a medium bowl, whisk together 2 egg whites, melted butter, vinegar, stevia, yeast mixture, and dissolved gelatin powder.

6 Stir egg mixture into dry ingredients and then stir in remaining ¼ cup boiling water.

7 Let batter rest 3 minutes to thicken. Divide batter into four equal parts and roll each into a ball. (Oil your hands if dough is sticky.) Place balls on an ungreased baking sheet.

8 In a small bowl, beat remaining egg white with a fork until foamy. Lightly brush onto bun tops. Sprinkle sesame seeds on top.

9 Bake about 30 minutes until buns are golden brown on top and bottom.

10 Turn off oven and let buns cool completely with oven door slightly ajar.

11 Serve immediately or store in a zip-top plastic bag in the refrigerator up to 1 week.

CHAPTER 13

DRINKS

SUN TEA

This is the method many of our grandmothers used to make iced tea in the summer, and it's a lost art. The main difference between Sun Tea and regular iced tea is that the water to make Sun Tea isn't boiled. Instead, tea bags are steeped in a glass jug outside in the sun until the tea reaches your desired strength.

Serves 8

8 black tea bags
1 gallon cool filtered water

Per Serving
Calories: 0 | Fat: 0g | Protein: 0g |
Sodium: 0mg | Fiber: 0g |
Carbohydrates: 0g |
Net Carbs: 0g | Sugar: 0g

1 In a gallon-sized glass jug with a lid, add tea bags and water.

2 Place jug outside in the sun and let it steep 2–4 hours until it reaches your desired strength.

3 Remove tea bags. Store tea in the refrigerator up to 1 week.

4 Serve over ice.

Do You Serve Sun Tea Sweetened?

Feel free to sweeten Sun Tea with your favorite keto sweetener. A liquid sweetener, such as liquid stevia, easily dissolves in the tea.

SWEET TEA

You will likely find this staple stashed away in a southerner's kitchen at any given point, just in case company pops by. Feel free to adjust the sweetener to suit your personal taste preference.

Serves 8

8 cups filtered water
4 black tea bags
½ cup granulated (or crystallized) allulose sweetener
8 slices fresh lemon
8 mint leaves

Per Serving
Calories: 5 | Fat: 0g | Protein: 0g | Sodium: 7mg | Fiber: 0g | Carbohydrates: 13g | Net Carbs: 1g | Sugar: 12g

1 In a medium saucepan over high heat, add water and bring to a boil.

2 Add tea bags and steep 3–5 minutes until tea reaches your desired strength.

3 Remove tea bags and stir in allulose.

4 Cool to room temperature, then refrigerate to chill. Store in the refrigerator up to 1 week.

5 To serve, dilute with water to taste. Serve over ice garnished with lemon and mint.

ARNOLD PALMER

There's no need to choose between two classic, favorite drinks! If you love Lemonade and Sweet Tea, the Arnold Palmer is for you. It combines them in one sweet and tangy beverage.

Serves 8

1 batch Lemonade (see recipe in this chapter)
½ batch Sweet Tea (see recipe in this chapter)

Per Serving
Calories: 8 | Fat: 0g | Protein: 0g | Sodium: 3mg | Fiber: 0g | Carbohydrates: 19g | Net Carbs: 1g | Sugar: 18g

1 In a large pitcher or jug, combine Lemonade and Sweet Tea.

2 Store in the refrigerator up to 1 week. Serve over ice.

LEMONADE

Nothing says refreshment quite like a cold glass of fresh lemonade! This recipe uses a quick simple syrup made with allulose. If you like your lemonade sweet but not too sweet, this will be perfect for you.

Serves 4

½ cup granulated (or crystallized) allulose sweetener
½ cup filtered water
½ cup fresh lemon juice
3 cups cold filtered water

Per Serving
Calories: 12 | Fat: 0g | Protein: 0g | Sodium: 0mg | Fiber: 0g | Carbohydrates: 26g | Net Carbs: 2g | Sugar: 25g

1 To make a simple syrup, in a small saucepan over medium heat, add allulose and ½ cup filtered water. Whisk about 1 minute until allulose is dissolved. Turn off heat and let cool to room temperature.

2 In a large pitcher, stir together simple syrup, fresh lemon juice, and 3 cups cold filtered water.

3 Store in the refrigerator up to 1 week.

4 Serve over ice.

Can You Make Lemonade with Lime Juice?

You can make this recipe with lime juice instead of lemon juice for a slightly different flavor. Also know that the macronutrient information will change slightly.

STRAWBERRY LEMONADE

(pictured)

If you like regular lemonade, you're sure to love the delicious sweet-tart flavor and beautiful color of Strawberry Lemonade! If you prefer, use fresh red raspberries instead of strawberries.

Serves 4

½ cup granulated (or crystallized) allulose sweetener
½ cup filtered water
½ cup fresh lemon juice
3 cups cold filtered water
½ cup hulled strawberries, muddled

1 To make a simple syrup, in a medium saucepan over medium heat, add allulose and ½ cup filtered water. Whisk about 1 minute until allulose is dissolved. Turn off heat and let cool to room temperature.

2 In a large pitcher, stir together simple syrup, lemon juice, 3 cups cold filtered water, and muddled strawberries.

3 Serve over ice. Can be stored in the refrigerator up to 1 week.

Per Serving

Calories: 19 | Fat: 0g | Protein: 0g | Sodium: 0mg | Fiber: 1g | Carbohydrates: 28g | Net Carbs: 3g | Sugar: 26g

STONE FRUIT SANGRIA MOCKTAILS

Traditional Spanish sangria usually features apples and oranges steeped in a combination of wine, brandy, and sugar. It's delicious and refreshing, but also very high in carbs. This version eliminates the carbs and the booze, but not the flavor!

Serves 8

1 batch Sweet Tea (see recipe in this chapter)
¼ cup pomegranate juice
2 small plums, pitted and thinly sliced
1 medium lemon, thinly sliced

In a large pitcher, stir together all ingredients. Serve over ice.

Per Serving

Calories: 16 | Fat: 0g | Protein: 0g | Sodium: 7mg | Fiber: 0g | Carbohydrates: 16g | Net Carbs: 4g | Sugar: 12g

MERMAID LEMONADE

Whether you call it Mermaid Lemonade *or* Unicorn Tea, *you're sure to love the magic that happens with this drink! Dried butterfly pea flowers are infused in water to form the base. The really fun part comes when you add acid, such as fresh lemon juice, to butterfly pea flower infusion—it changes color from blue to pink in varying shades depending on how much acid you add!*

Serves 4

4½ cups filtered water
¼ cup granulated (or crystallized) allulose sweetener
¼ cup dried butterfly pea flowers
4 lemon wedges
4 slices lemon
4 whole cherries

Per Serving
Calories: 10 | Fat: 0g | Protein: 0g |
Sodium: 2mg | Fiber: 0g |
Carbohydrates: 14g |
Net Carbs: 2g | Sugar: 13g

1 In a medium saucepan over medium heat, add water and allulose. Bring to a simmer and stir about 1 minute until allulose is dissolved.

2 Remove from heat, add butterfly pea flowers, and steep 5 minutes.

3 Strain infusion through a fine-mesh sieve and discard flowers. Cool syrup to room temperature, and then refrigerate 1 hour to chill.

4 Pour chilled butterfly pea flower infusion into four glasses with ice. Squeeze 1 lemon wedge into each glass, stir, and watch the color change.

5 Add 1 lemon slice and cherry to each glass and serve.

Try the Adult Version

If you're making this drink for folks who are twenty-one years and up, Mermaid Tea is great with a splash of white rum or vodka!

DARK AND STORMY MOCKTAILS

A classic Dark and Stormy is a cocktail made with ginger beer and dark rum served over ice garnished with fresh lime. In our keto version, a sweet ginger and lime infusion replaces the ginger beer, cutting out a significant amount of the carbs. Add 6 ounces dark rum to the pitcher if you want to make this an adult beverage!

Serves 4

1½ cups filtered water

½ cup sliced fresh ginger

½ cup chopped lime peel (peel only, as little of the white part as possible)

⅓ cup granulated (or crystallized) allulose sweetener

2 tablespoons fresh lime juice

2½ cups unflavored sparkling water

Per Serving

Calories: 5 | Fat: 0g | Protein: 0g | Sodium: 0mg | Fiber: 0g | Carbohydrates: 17g | Net Carbs: 1g | Sugar: 16g

1 In a medium saucepan over medium heat, add filtered water, ginger, lime peel, and allulose. Bring to a simmer and stir about 1 minute until allulose is dissolved. Remove from heat and let cool and infuse 1 hour. Strain infusion through a fine-mesh sieve and discard ginger and lime peel.

2 In a large pitcher, combine ginger-infused water with lime juice and sparkling water. Serve over ice.

Switch It Up with Fresh Herbs

Play around with the flavor profile of this recipe by adding fresh herbs to steep along with the ginger and lime peel. Fresh mint, basil, or lemongrass are all delicious, but feel free to experiment with what you like.

BLUE RASPBERRY "KOOL-AID"

As a wink and a nod to the bright-hued drinks of our youth, we made a real blue raspberry drink! Dried butterfly pea flowers, which are native to Southeast Asia, naturally make this beautiful drink blue.

Serves 4

4½ cups filtered water
¼ cup granulated (or crystallized) allulose sweetener
¼ cup dried butterfly pea flowers
3 drops raspberry extract
4 tablespoons fresh red raspberries

Per Serving
Calories: 12 | Fat: 0g |
Protein: 0g | Sodium: 2mg |
Fiber: 1g | Carbohydrates: 14g |
Net Carbs: 2g | Sugar: 12g

1 In a medium saucepan over medium heat, add water and allulose. Bring to a simmer and stir about 1 minute until allulose is dissolved.

2 Remove from heat, add butterfly pea flowers, and let steep 5 minutes.

3 Strain infusion through a fine-mesh sieve and discard flowers. Stir in raspberry extract.

4 Cool to room temperature and then refrigerate to chill.

5 Serve over ice, adding 1 tablespoon fresh raspberries to each glass.

Dried Butterfly Pea Flowers and Raspberry Extract

Dried butterfly pea flowers are available as a tisane (similar to a tea) in many Asian grocery stores and online. Raspberry extract can be found in specialty baking supply stores, sometimes in the baking aisle of regular grocery stores, or online.

CHAPTER 14

DESSERTS

GRILLED STRAWBERRY KEBABS

As far as summertime desserts go, anything with strawberries is a winner! Instead of taking the time to make something like strawberry shortcake or pound cake with strawberry sauce, cook up a few strawberries for dessert right on the grill! Not only does it save on carbs, but if you're cooking dinner on the grill anyway, it's minimal extra work.

Serves 4

20 medium strawberries, hulled
Coconut oil spray
⅛ teaspoon sea salt
2 tablespoons chopped fresh mint leaves, chiffonade style

Per Serving
Calories: 29 | Fat: 1g | Protein: 0g |
Sodium: 49mg | Fiber: 1g |
Carbohydrates: 5g | Net Carbs: 4g |
Sugar: 3g

1 Submerge four wooden skewers in water 20 minutes. Preheat grill to medium-high heat.

2 Thread 5 strawberries onto each skewer. Lightly spray strawberries with coconut oil.

3 Grill strawberries 2–4 minutes per side until lightly charred.

4 Transfer strawberry skewers to a platter and sprinkle with sea salt and fresh mint. Serve.

What Other Flavors Go Well with Grilled Strawberries?

This recipe is delicious with basil instead of mint! You can also use lime zest, or skip the mint and salt and drizzle a little Balsamic Glaze (see Chapter 4) on top.

CHOCOLATE CAKE WITH FUDGY GANACHE

Sometimes an occasion just requires cake! Just because you're following a keto diet doesn't mean you have to miss out. Whether it's a picnic, a potluck, or a birthday, this super-fudgy chocolate cake is a must-have.

Serves 16 (Makes a 2-layer 9" round cake)

CHOCOLATE CAKE

2 cups almond flour

¾ cup unsweetened cocoa powder

¼ cup ground golden flaxseed meal

2 teaspoons baking powder

½ teaspoon salt

¼ teaspoon baking soda

¾ cup unsalted butter, at room temperature

1 cup granulated (or crystallized) allulose sweetener

4 large eggs

¾ cup whole milk

1 tablespoon pure vanilla extract

1 teaspoon instant espresso powder, dissolved in 2 teaspoons hot water

FUDGY GANACHE

2 ounces 90% cocoa dark chocolate

¼ cup unsalted butter

¼ cup heavy whipping cream

20 drops liquid stevia

½ teaspoon pure vanilla extract

⅛ teaspoon salt

2 tablespoons powdered erythritol

1 *For the Chocolate Cake:* Preheat oven to 350°F.

2 Rub coconut oil inside two (9") round cake pans. Dust with coconut flour and shake it around inside the pans to coat. Trim two pieces of parchment paper to fit inside the bottom of pans; place in pans and lightly spray paper with coconut oil spray.

3 In a large bowl, whisk together almond flour, cocoa powder, flaxseed meal, baking powder, salt, and baking soda.

4 In a separate large bowl, beat together butter and allulose until creamy. Then beat in eggs, milk, vanilla, and dissolved espresso.

5 Beat the dry ingredients into the wet ingredients just until combined.

6 Divide batter between prepared cake pans, spreading it out evenly.

7 Bake about 30 minutes until a toothpick inserted into cakes comes out with just a couple of crumbs, rotating pans once halfway through.

8 Cool cakes 30 minutes in pans, then turn them out onto wire racks to finish cooling. Let cakes cool completely before frosting.

9 *For the Fudgy Ganache:* In a double boiler or microwave, melt together dark chocolate and butter.

10 In a medium bowl, whisk all remaining ingredients with melted chocolate.

Per Serving

Calories: 274 | Fat: 24g |
Protein: 7g | Sodium: 198mg |
Fiber: 4g | Carbohydrates: 21g |
Net Carbs: 4g | Sugar: 14g

11 Cool to room temperature and then frost the cake. Let frosting set before slicing and serving.

12 Store frosted cake covered in the refrigerator up to 1 week.

BLACKBERRY-COCONUT SORBET

(pictured)

With its deep-purple color, this sweet, tart, refreshing sorbet is the perfect way to cool down on a hot day! Feel free to garnish with some keto toppings such as a couple of fresh blackberries and a sprinkle of unsweetened coconut if you want.

Serves 4

2 cups frozen blackberries

½ cup canned unsweetened full-fat coconut milk

3 tablespoons granulated (or crystallized) allulose sweetener, dissolved in 2 tablespoons boiling water and cooled

1 teaspoon fresh lime zest

¹⁄₁₆ teaspoon sea salt

1 Add all ingredients to a blender and process until smooth and creamy, stopping to scrape sides as necessary.

2 For soft serve–style ice cream, serve immediately.

3 For hard ice cream, freeze 2 hours before serving.

Per Serving

Calories: 88 | Fat: 6g | Protein: 2g | Sodium: 28mg | Fiber: 4g | Carbohydrates: 17g | Net Carbs: 4g | Sugar: 13g

---

WATERMELON WITH BALSAMIC GLAZE

This is one of our favorite ways to enjoy watermelon. The Balsamic Glaze adds the perfect amount of tang to balance the fruit's sweetness.

Serves 4

3 cups cubed watermelon

Avocado oil spray

4 teaspoons Balsamic Glaze (see Chapter 4)

Per Serving

Calories: 53 | Fat: 1g | Protein: 1g | Sodium: 27mg | Fiber: 0g | Carbohydrates: 13g | Net Carbs: 10g | Sugar: 12g

1 Submerge four wooden skewers in water 20 minutes. Preheat grill to medium-high heat.

2 Thread watermelon onto skewers. Lightly spray with avocado oil.

3 Grill watermelon skewers 2–3 minutes on one side and 1–2 minutes on the other side until grill marks appear on both sides.

4 Drizzle on Balsamic Glaze. Serve.

RASPBERRY CRISP

If you're looking for a new dessert idea that's perfect for bringing to any summer gathering, look no further. The only thing that would make this Raspberry Crisp even better is topping it with a dollop of freshly whipped cream!

Serves 8

CRUMBLE TOPPING

6 tablespoons unsalted butter, at room temperature

4 tablespoons granulated monk fruit–erythritol blend

1½ teaspoons pure vanilla extract

¼ plus ⅛ teaspoon salt

1½ cups almond flour

1 cup unsweetened shredded coconut

RASPBERRY FILLING

10 ounces unsweetened frozen red raspberries

4 tablespoons granulated (or crystallized) allulose sweetener

1 teaspoon fresh lemon juice

¹⁄₁₆ teaspoon salt

Per Serving

Calories: 303 | Fat: 25g | Protein: 6g | Sodium: 128mg | Fiber: 7g | Carbohydrates: 20g | Net Carbs: 4g | Sugar: 9g | Sugar Alcohol: 3g

1. *For the Crumble Topping:* In a large bowl, using an electric mixer on medium speed, cream together butter and monk fruit–erythritol, then beat in vanilla and salt. Stir in almond flour and then shredded coconut.

2. *For the Raspberry Filling:* In a large bowl, stir together raspberries, allulose, lemon juice, and salt.

3. Preheat oven to 375°F.

4. Pour Raspberry Filling into an ungreased 9" pie pan and spread out evenly. Sprinkle Crumble Topping evenly on top.

5. Bake 25–35 minutes until bubbling along the outside and crust is golden on top. Serve warm.

Can You Skip the Coconut?

Yes! You can omit the coconut in the topping and leave everything else the same. Or add up to 1 cup chopped nuts instead!

BERRY CRUMBLE BARS

This sweet treat is perfect for when you're craving summer fruit and it's not summertime; frozen berries are the star of the show! And of course you'd never know they're frozen. These bars are sweet, nutty, and bursting with berry flavor. If you want to use fresh berries, just use 3 cups fresh mixed berries and add ¼ cup water.

Serves 12

CRUST

6 tablespoons unsalted butter, at room temperature

4 tablespoons granulated monk fruit–erythritol blend

1½ teaspoons pure vanilla extract

¼ plus ⅛ teaspoon salt

1½ cups almond flour

MIXED BERRY FILLING

3 cups unsweetened frozen mixed berries (strawberries, blueberries, blackberries, raspberries)

3 tablespoons granulated (or crystallized) allulose sweetener

2 tablespoons chia seeds

1/16 teaspoon salt

TOPPING

½ cup pecans, coarsely chopped

2 tablespoons almond flour

½ teaspoon ground cinnamon

Per Serving

Calories: 124 | Fat: 10g |
Protein: 1g | Sodium: 86mg |
Fiber: 3g | Carbohydrates: 12g |
Net Carbs: 4g | Sugar: 6g |
Sugar Alcohol: 2g

1 *For the Crust:* Preheat oven to 325°F. Line an 8" × 8" glass dish with parchment paper.

2 In a large bowl, using an electric mixer on medium speed, cream together butter and monk fruit–erythritol, then beat in vanilla, salt, and almond flour.

3 Press three-fourths of dough evenly into the bottom and about ½" up the sides of prepared dish, using a metal spatula to flatten it. Reserve the other one-fourth dough for Topping.

4 Bake 20–25 minutes until light golden.

5 *For the Mixed Berry Filling:* In a medium saucepan over medium heat, add berries and allulose. Cook covered 10 minutes, and then remove lid and cook uncovered an additional 2 minutes, stirring occasionally.

6 Turn off heat and whisk in chia seeds and salt. Mash berries with a potato masher to a chunky consistency.

7 Pour berry filling into prebaked crust.

8 *For the Topping:* In a small bowl, use a fork to combine the reserved one-fourth of crust dough with pecans, almond flour, and cinnamon until it looks crumbly. Sprinkle this mixture on top of berry filling.

9 Bake 15–20 minutes until filling is set along the outside and top is golden.

10 Serve warm, at room temperature, or chilled. Store leftovers covered in refrigerator up to 3 days.

GRASSHOPPER PIE BARS

If you're a fan of the chocolate-peppermint flavor combination, this one will be a winner in your book! Take it up a notch and top it with freshly whipped cream and dark chocolate shavings.

Serves 12

CHOCOLATE CRUST

¼ cup unsalted butter, at room temperature

3 tablespoons granulated monk fruit–erythritol blend

1 teaspoon pure vanilla extract

3 drops stevia glycerite

¼ teaspoon salt

1 cup almond flour

2 tablespoons unsweetened cocoa powder

MINT CUSTARD

1 cup heavy whipping cream

¼ cup water

⅓ cup granulated (or crystallized) allulose sweetener

⅛ teaspoon salt

8 large egg yolks

¾ teaspoon beef gelatin powder

2 tablespoons boiling water

1 teaspoon pure vanilla extract

1 teaspoon peppermint extract

⅛ teaspoon stevia glycerite

Per Serving

Calories: 207 | Fat: 19g |
Protein: 5g | Sodium: 87mg |
Fiber: 1g | Carbohydrates: 10g |
Net Carbs: 3g | Sugar: 6g |
Sugar Alcohol: 2g

1 *For the Chocolate Crust:* Preheat oven to 325°F. Line an 8" × 6" glass dish with parchment paper.

2 In a large bowl, using an electric mixer on medium speed, cream together butter and monk fruit–erythritol, then beat in vanilla, stevia, salt, almond flour, and cocoa powder.

3 Press dough evenly into prepared dish, using a metal spatula to flatten it.

4 Bake 25–30 minutes until set but not hard. Cool to room temperature.

5 *For the Mint Custard:* In a medium saucepan over medium heat, add cream, water, allulose, and salt. Heat until mixture is steaming and starting to bubble around the outside.

6 In a medium bowl, add egg yolks. Whisk 1 cup scalded cream mixture into egg yolks, starting with just a couple of drops at first and gradually whisking in the entire 1 cup.

7 Pour tempered egg yolk mixture back into cream mixture. Reduce heat to low and cook about 5–10 minutes until boiling, stirring constantly. Immediately remove from heat.

8 In a small bowl, combine gelatin powder and boiling water and stir to dissolve.

9 Whisk dissolved gelatin powder, vanilla, peppermint, and stevia into cream mixture until smooth.

10 Strain custard through a fine-mesh sieve; discard solids.

11 Pour strained custard into prebaked crust. Cover and refrigerate about 4 hours until custard is set.

12 Serve or store covered in the refrigerator up to 5 days.

BANANA CREAM PIE BARS

Banana custard in a sweet, buttery crust reminds us of the summer potlucks of our youth! Add a dollop of whipped cream and a sprinkle of chopped nuts to make it pretty (and even more delicious).

Serves 12

CRUST

¼ cup unsalted butter, at room temperature

3 tablespoons granulated monk fruit–erythritol blend

1 teaspoon pure vanilla extract

¼ teaspoon salt

1 cup almond flour

BANANA CUSTARD

1 cup heavy whipping cream

¼ cup water

⅓ cup granulated (or crystallized) allulose sweetener

⅛ teaspoon salt

8 large egg yolks

¾ teaspoon beef gelatin powder

2 tablespoons boiling water

1 teaspoon pure vanilla extract

1 teaspoon banana extract

⅛ teaspoon stevia glycerite

Per Serving

Calories: 205 | Fat: 18g | Protein: 5g | Sodium: 86mg | Fiber: 1g | Carbohydrates: 10g | Net Carbs: 3g | Sugar: 6g | Sugar Alcohol: 2g

1 *For the Crust:* Preheat oven to 325°F. Line an 8" × 6" glass dish with parchment paper.

2 In a large bowl, using an electric mixer on medium speed, cream together butter and monk fruit–erythritol, then beat in vanilla, salt, and almond flour.

3 Press dough evenly into the prepared dish, using a metal spatula to flatten it.

4 Bake 25–30 minutes until light golden. Cool to room temperature.

5 *For the Banana Custard:* In a medium saucepan over medium heat, add cream, water, allulose, and salt. Heat until steaming and starting to bubble around the outside.

6 In a medium bowl, add egg yolks. Whisk 1 cup scalded cream mixture to egg yolks, starting with just a couple of drops at first and gradually whisking in the entire 1 cup.

7 Pour tempered egg yolk mixture back into cream mixture. Reduce heat to low and cook until boiling, stirring constantly. Immediately remove from heat.

8 In a small bowl, combine gelatin powder and boiling water and stir to dissolve.

9 Whisk dissolved gelatin powder, vanilla, banana extract, and stevia into cream mixture until smooth.

10 Strain custard through a fine-mesh sieve; discard solids.

11 Pour strained custard into prebaked crust. Cover and refrigerate about 4 hours until custard is set.

12 Serve or store covered in the refrigerator up to 5 days.

RED, WHITE, AND BLUE BERRY PARFAITS

If you're looking for a great patriotic summer treat, these parfaits will become your new go-to! To make them ahead of time, assemble them without adding the crumbled Shortbread Bars and add them just before serving. For the yogurt, we use FAGE Total 5% Milkfat Greek Yogurt, which is readily available at grocery stores.

Serves 6

STRAWBERRY JAM

1½ cups whole strawberries, hulled

4 teaspoons granulated monk fruit–erythritol blend

¹⁄₁₆ teaspoon salt

YOGURT CREAM

1 cup unsweetened plain whole milk Greek yogurt

2 tablespoons granulated monk fruit–erythritol blend

½ teaspoon pure vanilla extract

⅔ cup heavy whipping cream, whipped to stiff peaks

TOPPING

3 Shortbread Bars squares, crumbled (see recipe in this chapter)

6 tablespoons fresh blueberries

Per Serving

Calories: 132 | Fat: 9g |
Protein: 5g | Sodium: 74mg |
Fiber: 2g | Carbohydrates: 12g |
Net Carbs: 7g | Sugar: 5g |
Sugar Alcohol: 3g

1 *For the Strawberry Jam:* In a medium bowl, add all ingredients to a bowl and mash with a fork to a chunky consistency. Set aside.

2 *For the Yogurt Cream:* In a medium bowl, beat together yogurt, monk fruit–erythritol, and vanilla. Add whipped cream one-fourth at a time, stirring gently after each addition.

3 Place 1 tablespoon Strawberry Jam in the bottom of each of six individual parfait glasses.

4 Divide Yogurt Cream evenly among glasses.

5 Divide remaining Strawberry Jam evenly among glasses and spoon on top.

6 Top with crumbled Shortbread Bars.

7 Add 1 tablespoon fresh blueberries to top of each parfait. Serve.

SHORTBREAD BARS

Crisp, buttery, and perfectly sweet, these Shortbread Bars are sure to be a hit at your next party or gathering! If you want to play around with the flavor profile, feel free to add up to ½ cup of any of the following: stevia-sweetened chocolate chips, chopped pecans, or unsweetened shredded coconut.

Serves 8

¼ cup unsalted butter, at room temperature

4 tablespoons granulated monk fruit–erythritol blend

1 teaspoon pure vanilla extract

¼ teaspoon salt

1 cup almond flour

Per Serving

Calories: 145 | Fat: 13g |
Protein: 3g | Sodium: 73mg |
Fiber: 2g | Carbohydrates: 6g |
Net Carbs: 1g | Sugar: 1g |
Sugar Alcohol: 3g

1 Preheat oven to 325°F. Line an 8" × 6" glass dish with parchment paper.

2 In a large bowl, using an electric mixer on medium speed, cream together butter and monk fruit–erythritol, then beat in vanilla, salt, and almond flour.

3 Press dough evenly into prepared dish, using a metal spatula to flatten it.

4 Bake 25–30 minutes until golden.

5 Cool 2 hours before cutting to give shortbread time to harden and become crisp. Cut into sixteen squares.

6 Store covered at room temperature up to 5 days.

How to Recrisp These Cookies

If it's humid out, these cookies can lose their crunch a bit. They recrisp well in a 325°F oven for about 10 minutes. Watch them carefully so they don't get too dark!

PECAN PIE BARS

You're going to be surprised at how much these Pecan Pie Bars taste like a real-deal pecan pie! Feel free to drizzle on a little dark chocolate to make them extra decadent. And save the recipe for the holidays!

Serves 12

CRUST

¼ cup unsalted butter, at room temperature

3 tablespoons granulated monk fruit–erythritol blend

1 teaspoon pure vanilla extract

¼ teaspoon salt

1 cup almond flour

PECAN FILLING

6 tablespoons unsalted butter

5 tablespoons granulated (or crystallized) allulose sweetener

¼ teaspoon salt

1½ teaspoons pure vanilla extract

6 tablespoons heavy whipping cream

2 large eggs, lightly whisked

1 cup pecans, lightly toasted

Per Serving

Calories: 244 | Fat: 23g | Protein: 4g | Sodium: 112mg | Fiber: 2g | Carbohydrates: 10g | Net Carbs: 2g | Sugar: 6g

1 *For the Crust:* Preheat oven to 325°F. Line an 8" × 6" glass dish with parchment paper.

2 In a large bowl, using an electric mixer on medium speed, cream together butter and monk fruit–erythritol, then beat in vanilla, salt, and almond flour.

3 Press dough evenly into prepared dish, using a metal spatula to flatten it.

4 Bake 15–20 minutes until light golden.

5 *For the Pecan Filling:* In a medium saucepan over medium heat, add butter, allulose, and salt. Cook until it reaches a boil, then boil 1 minute, whisking frequently.

6 Turn off heat and whisk in vanilla, cream, and eggs. Stir in pecans.

7 Pour pecan filling mixture onto prebaked crust. Bake about 15 minutes until filling is set along the outside and crust is golden.

8 Cool to room temperature and then slice and serve or store covered in refrigerator up to 5 days.

Standard US/Metric Measurement Conversions

VOLUME CONVERSIONS	
US Volume Measure	**Metric Equivalent**
⅛ teaspoon	0.5 milliliter
¼ teaspoon	1 milliliter
½ teaspoon	2 milliliters
1 teaspoon	5 milliliters
½ tablespoon	7 milliliters
1 tablespoon (3 teaspoons)	15 milliliters
2 tablespoons (1 fluid ounce)	30 milliliters
¼ cup (4 tablespoons)	60 milliliters
⅓ cup	90 milliliters
½ cup (4 fluid ounces)	125 milliliters
⅔ cup	160 milliliters
¾ cup (6 fluid ounces)	180 milliliters
1 cup (16 tablespoons)	250 milliliters
1 pint (2 cups)	500 milliliters
1 quart (4 cups)	1 liter (about)
WEIGHT CONVERSIONS	
US Weight Measure	**Metric Equivalent**
½ ounce	15 grams
1 ounce	30 grams
2 ounces	60 grams
3 ounces	85 grams
¼ pound (4 ounces)	115 grams
½ pound (8 ounces)	225 grams
¾ pound (12 ounces)	340 grams
1 pound (16 ounces)	454 grams

OVEN TEMPERATURE CONVERSIONS

Degrees Fahrenheit	Degrees Celsius
200 degrees F	95 degrees C
250 degrees F	120 degrees C
275 degrees F	135 degrees C
300 degrees F	150 degrees C
325 degrees F	160 degrees C
350 degrees F	180 degrees C
375 degrees F	190 degrees C
400 degrees F	205 degrees C
425 degrees F	220 degrees C
450 degrees F	230 degrees C

BAKING PAN SIZES

American	Metric
8 × 1½ inch round baking pan	20 × 4 cm cake tin
9 × 1½ inch round baking pan	23 × 3.5 cm cake tin
11 × 7 × 1½ inch baking pan	28 × 18 × 4 cm baking tin
13 × 9 × 2 inch baking pan	30 × 20 × 5 cm baking tin
2 quart rectangular baking dish	30 × 20 × 3 cm baking tin
15 × 10 × 2 inch baking pan	30 × 25 × 2 cm baking tin (Swiss roll tin)
9 inch pie plate	22 × 4 or 23 × 4 cm pie plate
7 or 8 inch springform pan	18 or 20 cm springform or loose bottom cake tin
9 × 5 × 3 inch loaf pan	23 × 13 × 7 cm or 2 lb narrow loaf or pâté tin
1½ quart casserole	1.5 liter casserole
2 quart casserole	2 liter casserole

Index

H

I

J

K

L

M

Stick to Your Keto Diet **WITHOUT** Giving Up Your Favorite Foods!

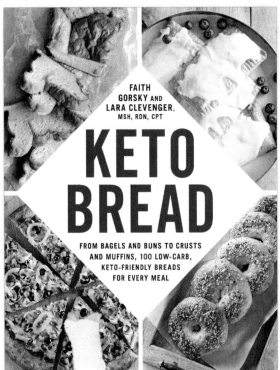

Pick Up or Download Your Copies Today!